integrating the biblical message with everyday realities. Both clergy and lay persons will find this an invaluable resource.

Rev. Albert Cutié,
priest, author and talk-show host (Episcopal Diocese of
Southeast Florida)

Robert LaRochelle has written a sermon series that is a wonderful tool for both clergy and laity. He uses a positive and uplifting theology to address difficult issues facing the Church and Christians today. It is an excellent resource to aid in starting the conversations that our souls need to have. Rev. LaRochelle also provides a "dialogue sermon" format if you have never tried this!

Rev. Shauna Hyde
Christ Church United Methodist, Charleston, WV, author
of *Fifty Shades of Grace* and *Victim No More!*

LaRochelle has led by example in returning the sermon to its proper context in the liturgy of the church. However, here liturgy takes on its true meaning – the work of the people. This exploration of the communal and conversational nature of preaching will be helpful to any preacher looking for fresh eyes to see, ears to hear, and a mouth to preach Sunday's sermon.

Dr. Geoffrey Lentz,
First United Methodist Church, Port St. Joe, FL,
author *The Gospel According to St. Luke:A Participatory Study Guide* and *Learning and Living Scripture*, editor of *The Living Psalter*

PRAISE FOR *SO MUCH OLDER THEN* ...

In *So Much Older Then* ..., Robert Larochelle offers preachers a model for truly dialogical preaching. Most preaching takes the form of a monologue, even so called dialogical and conversational preaching is more about style than substance, but with this book preachers hear the invitation to step out of our comfort zone and invite the congregation to raise questions and enter a true conversation about the Word that has been proclaimed from the pulpit. The eight sermons in the series focus on the kinds of questions the author has been asked during the course of his ministry, questions about issues that range from the problem of suffering to the nature of faith itself. Although in some ways directed to preachers, this brief collection will prove valuable to any number of congregational conversations.

Dr. Bob Cornwall,
Central Woodward Christian Church,
author of *Unfettered Spirit: Spiritual Gifts for the Great Awakening* and *Faith in the Public Square*

So Much Older Then ... starts with a few lines from a Bob Dylan song. In the eight sermons that make up the book, the Reverend LaRochelle blends Jesus and Dylan, faith and intellect, individual salvation and community connectedness into a rich mix which challenges the mind and nourishes the soul. In this world of fragmented organized religion in which so many "true believers" are convinced that they have discovered the true path, Dr. LaRochelle's open invitation to worship – "All are welcome" – is a breath of theological fresh air. Raised a Roman Catholic and ordained a minister of the United Church of Christ, Bob's central message is clear – IT ALL COMES DOWN TO JESUS. Whatever your faith, whatever your theological pedigree, the compassion, acceptance, sacrifice, and connectedness with others displayed by Jesus is a model for humans of all faiths.

The most wonderful thing about Dr. LaRochelle's sermons is that he does not tell you what to believe. He draws you into thinking about what you believe and helps you work out your own basis for faith. In a world too often filled with religious absolutes, Dr. LaRochelle is a voice of reason and belief, of science and religion. Dr. LaRochelle speaks of the teachings of Jesus as a foundation for connectedness, creating a bond between and among us. The personal thinking generated by reading his sermons left me with the revelation that, for me, God is that which is in between, that which connects us with everyone and everything – the celestial glue, if you will. Perhaps it is really possible to be a scientific Druid, love Jesus, and respect the faith of others. Like many, I was taught in a tradition of religious certainty, but I'm younger than that now.

Dr. Curtis Brand,
author, musician, clinical psychologist

So Much Older Then ... is not only a genuinely loving tribute to Rev. LaRochelle's former congregation, but an inspiring reflection upon the questions we have all faced. The Reverend presents to us a collection of sermons and congregational responses in which the reader can clearly detect the passion and care with which they were originally delivered. The appeal in LaRochelle's writing rests not in his answers to the burning questions of life, but in his ability to unearth even deeper queries, forcing the reader to more carefully explore his or her faith. This book is a must-read for everyone, regardless of where you may be along your spiritual journey.

Eric R. Hutchinson,
Songwriter/Composer (*Believer: The Musical, Lullabies and Love Songs*, Imagine Stage Productions)

In *So Much Older Then ...*, Rev. Bob LaRochelle offers us a series of inspiring sermons based on the Sacred Scriptures and on the real-life struggles of those he has been privileged to serve in various congregations. The discussion questions are especially helpful in

So Much Older Then ...

Understanding Preaching as Conversation

Robert LaRochelle

Energion Publications
Gonzalez, FL
2013

Cover Design: Henry Neufeld
Background Picture: © Kathie Nichols
Dreamstime.com
http://www.dreamstime.com/kathienichols_info

ISBN13: 978-1-938434-51-8
ISBN10: 1-938434-51-X

Library of Congress Control Number: 2013933883

Energion Publications
P. O. Box 841
Gonzalez, FL 32560

energionpubs.com

'Yes, my guard stood hard when abstract threats
Too noble to neglect
Deceived me into thinking
I had something to protect
Good and bad, I define these terms
Quite clear, no doubt, somehow
Ah, but I was so much older then
I'm younger than that now'
    'My Back Pages' – Bob Dylan

DEDICATION

I am so pleased to dedicate this book to the members and friends of the Congregational Church of Union, Connecticut, United Church of Christ. It was in this congregation, which I served from early 2001 to the middle of 2012, that I preached the sermon series around which this book is centered. I dedicate this book to these wonderful people in gratitude for their openness to God's Word and for the many ways in which they proclaimed that Word to me.

ACKNOWLEDGMENTS

Along with my former congregation, the Congregational Church of Union, Connecticut, UCC, to whom this book is dedicated, there are several other individuals I wish to acknowledge. First and foremost is my wife, Patricia Coppinger LaRochelle. She has not only sat through many of my sermons in church sanctuaries, but she has also witnessed patiently as many of their ideas have unfolded at home. Likewise, our three children, Brian, Kathleen and Stephen, have quite often shared in their mom's situation. Quite seriously – For all of their insights and feedback, I am most grateful and I acknowledge these four special people in my life with my undying and ever abiding love!

I also wish to thank my new congregation, the Second Congregational Church, Manchester, Connecticut, UCC, for their willingness to call me to serve them as their pastor. I am deeply grateful for the relationships we are forming together and eagerly anticipate the many opportunities that lie ahead where we can share in our common 'priesthood of believers.' For the ways in which this church has dedicated itself to living out the message of Jesus both within and beyond our walls, I am greatly inspired.

Finally, I am most thankful for the ministry of Henry and Jody Neufeld, whose commitment to Christian publishing and to seeking common ground among believers is truly exemplary. In particular, I thank Henry for his outstanding support as I have written both this book and my previous one, *Crossing the Street.* It is my hope that through these published words, you and I, writer and reader, may grow in a far more important task—to be hearers and doers of the Word of God, the very Word made manifest in Jesus!

South Windsor, Connecticut
October 31, 2012
Reformation Day

TABLE OF CONTENTS

Acknowledgments v
Introduction.. 1
Chapter One 7
Chapter Two 19
Chapter Three 31
Chapter Four... 41
Chapter Five.. 49
Chapter Six 55
Chapter Seven 63
Chapter Eight 69
Conclusion: So Much Older Then.. 77

INTRODUCTION

Each and every Sunday in churches throughout the world, members of local congregations sit in their seats and listen to a message that has traditionally gone by the name 'sermon.'[1] Suffice it to say that this message is such a vital part of worship that many people evaluate the attractiveness of a particular church by the quality of the preaching one experiences within it. Throughout the course of my career as an ordained minister in both Protestant and Catholic churches,[2] I have preached hundreds of times. On certain occasions and for particular reasons, I have moved away from the traditional approach wherein the preacher speaks and the congregation listens. Instead, I have delivered a message on that particular morning and provided time right after it for members of the congregation to respond with questions or comments if they decided to do so. It is from an extended period of time wherein I took such an approach that the idea behind this book was born.

Within the pages of what you are now reading, you will find eight sermons. That's not all you will find here but they will form the centerpiece for each of the chapters you will read. These sermons were preached as part of a series in the summer of 2012 in the Congregational Church of Union, Connecticut, United Church of Christ, where I had served for over eleven years by the time this series started.

What is unique about this particular series is that each of my messages was a bit shorter than that which you might hear on most Sundays at my church. The reason for my relative brevity (and it is relative indeed!) is that at the end of each message, I 'open up the floor' and encourage members of the congregation to react

---

1   In some traditions, e.g. Roman Catholicism, this is known by the title 'homily.'

2   I was ordained a United Church of Christ clergyperson in 2002. I served as a Permanent Deacon in the Catholic Church from 1989-1998

back to the sermon-to, as mentioned above, ask questions, make comments, offer feedback, and possibly even critique something I either said or didn't say!

It is important to know that I preach in the 'traditional' style over ninety percent of the time. Yet, over the course of my pastorate in that church, I sought to develop opportunities such as the one described here for two basic reasons, one highly theological, the other what we might call pastoral.

Let's start with the theological: As Christian believers, we contend that the Word of God as contained within the Scriptures is 'living and active'[1] and that it has the power to touch the heart and to inspire each of us who read and hear it. In the long standing tradition of homiletics[2] within the Christian church, we have also contended that it is the task of the preacher to 'break open' the Word of God so as to facilitate this process. In simpler terms, I like to think of preaching as structuring a message in such a way that in effect the preacher actually gets out of God's way as both God and the hearer interact with one another during this time in the service in which the Word is so explicitly proclaimed.

As believers, we also affirm the reality of our shared 'priesthood.'[3] We recognize that God works in and through each of us and that we all have a message to share. In some traditions, such as my own, this recognition forms the basis for preaching by those who are not ordained on days such as designated Laity Sundays as well as other occasions.

Each time a preacher preaches, things are happening inside of the minds and the spirits of each person who is listening. Here is where what we might call a pastoral understanding enters into our discussion. What you and I hear in a sermon may be highly contingent upon where we happen to be in our life situations at the

---

1   Hebrews 4:12
2   The technical term for the study of preaching.
3   This is the concept of the 'priesthood of all believers,' a core concept of the Reformation. The Second Vatican Council of the Catholic Church refers to a 'priesthood of the faithful.' The concept is based on 1 Peter 2:9

very moment this sermon is preached. As I write these words, I am preparing next Sunday's message which centers on Jesus' discussion with the Pharisees about marriage and divorce. How His words and mine are heard this coming Sunday morning and what they trigger in each hearer are greatly dependent upon the experiences with this topic each is reflecting upon at the particular time the sermon will be preached. One hearer may be worried about the possibility of divorce, another experiencing a custody battle, still another on the brink of committing to a new relationship, someone else coming off the high of one's honeymoon and not even prepared to imagine how so blissful a relationship could ever actually rupture.

All of which brings us back to the underlying theological assumptions I make. If we contend that each Christian believer has a message to share, why should we not provide opportunity for him/her to share it within the context of the local church's weekly gathering event, the service of worship? In using this approach over a period of several years, I have been deeply touched by what people have said when given the opportunity, by the questions my words led them to ponder and how the sharing of those questions made major contributions to the spiritual lives of THEIR hearers, including me!

This book is the result of something new for me. It is the first time I have used this preaching format in an extended sermon series. The sermons you read here were delivered over an eight week period during the months of July and August. In fact, this series itself is also the result of more than one new thing! In selecting the TOPICS for each of these shared messages, I opted to look at the kinds of QUESTIONS I have been asked in my life as a pastor and I tried to hone in on some of the recurring themes found therein. In this way, I felt I was preaching within the context of real life issues that had emerged within the lives of many of my listeners, several of whom articulated their questions to me.

Having done my doctoral work in the field of preaching, I was excited about this opportunity to put these beliefs I have expressed into practice over the period of several weeks. I also concluded early on that the process would be worth even more developed systematic reflection on my part. I was likewise hopeful that the result of this reflection would be of some value to others who are interested in both preaching and in the varied dynamics inherent in spiritual life wherever two, three or more are gathered. Hence, this book!

In each of the eight chapters that follow, you will find a similar format. I will begin by introducing some background to the question(s) about which I will be preaching. You will then have the opportunity to read my sermon as I wrote it. While I do speak aloud most of the words you will find printed, my written pulpit texts are not literal transcriptions of what I said from the pulpit on those summer mornings. On more than one occasion, I used the text as a springboard from which I gave examples that occurred to me at that moment. I find it important to say to you, the reader, that the sermon is different from the essay. The sermonic event is intended to be HEARD. It is not an essay to be read. Consequently, the preacher must craft it in such a way that it may make for clearer hearing. As a result, reading from these sermon notes is something that you may find to be quite difficult. So, as best you can, as you are reading these sermons, please try your very best to imagine them being delivered! In doing so, please recognize that these short phrases were delivered with the intention that the pacing of their delivery would be conducive to the hearer's ability to absorb the words of the message. Simply put, each sermon is a message to be delivered through the unique means of communication that constitutes what we call a sermon. What might read more clearly in essay form might very well fail in a preaching context which is part of a service of worship!

At the end of each chapter, I also include discussion questions that I am hoping will be of value to you, the reader. Ideally, this book will be a resource for ongoing conversation and reflection upon the proclaimed Word expressed in these pages. In that way, what was a summer sermonic moment in Union, Connecticut continues to be living and active in the unfolding of the reader's daily life, wherever she or he may be.

The questions selected for this sermon series represent real life human religious concerns as expressed to me a pastor over the course of several years, by people of different ages. In their selection, I recognized that I had identified a certain universality in the questions. These are issues that, while expressed by certain individuals, are hardly unique to those individuals alone and, in most cases, have been issues about which a considerable amount of theological and pastoral writing has been done over the years.

The series begins in Chapter One with the age old issue of why people suffer. Connected with this, Chapter Two explores how prayer fits into that question and what, in fact, the real purpose and effects of prayer might be. Chapter Three moves in a different direction as it considers the very future of faith in a pluralistic and changing world. Chapter Four delves more deeply into the very nature of who God is, which, of course, is connected to the matter of what, in fact, God does and has been doing for a very long time.

The occasion of a baptism in our congregation forms the basis for the sermon around which Chapter Five is centered. The fundamental question of where religion itself fits into human life and how so many religious approaches came to be is our matter for consideration in Chapter Six. Chapter Seven takes a different turn as I reflect upon the many questions I have been asked about what it's like to be an ordained minister and move from those questions to a homiletic reflection on the priesthood of all believers. Chapter Eight contains the final sermon in the series, the one which deals with the ultimate question of what might possibly happen to us when these days of our earthly life are over, something we clergy are asked about quite often and which forms the basis for discussions within families as well as with our friends.

The reader should be aware that a funny thing happened on my way to the end of this series. Toward the end of the month of July, just prior to the preaching of the fourth sermon in this series, I received and accepted a call to be the pastor of a new church, thus positioning myself to leave this beloved congregation I had served for these nearly 11 ½ truly wonderful years. Consequently, this series took on a new tone. It became a series of shared reflections that played an integral role in this process of transition, both for me and the congregation. As it worked out, my final service in this congregation was delivered two weeks following the conclusion of this series.

You will notice that as we move toward the end of the series, some moments of poignancy clearly occur. What may be less apparent is the internal sense of urgency I felt as I drew closer to this moment of leaving. As I reread and reviewed these sermons I had written, I recalled this internal drive I was feeling, this deep desire to be clear about what I wanted to tell these people I loved so dearly, this need I felt to do the best I could to, yes, get out of God's way and simply allow the Word to be alive in those who hear it.

A final note: If you are wondering about this title SO MUCH OLDER THEN and the epigraph you may have noticed before you started reading this Introduction, I am hoping that as you read the concluding chapter when you draw near the end of this book, that somehow the title might contribute to what you have discovered about yourself in these pages. I am also hopeful that, in your reading of these messages and your own reflection upon the conversations I describe, you will consider sharing your own thoughts with me as together we seek to both hear God's word and to apply it to our very lives![1]

---

1   You may send a note to me by going to www.facebook.com/
    somucholderthen, by contacting the publisher, pubs@energion.com, by
    contacting me directly rpbksl@gmail.com, or by sending me a message
    through Twitter @REVDRBOBL

CHAPTER ONE

Deciding where to begin this series of sermons was not particularly difficult. Of all the questions I have been asked as a pastor, the ones that seem most difficult and troubling are those that deal with why people suffer. Even more difficult are the questions about the suffering of the 'innocent,' those who have clearly done nothing wrong to 'deserve' their fate or who, to the contrary, live lives that represent the very epitome of goodness. The examples are all too abundant and any of us who have minimal access to television, newspaper or any form of information technology are quite familiar with tales of hurricane and tornado victims, hit and run accidents, and those stories of sudden death among individuals presumed to be healthy and in the very prime of their lives. Not long before this book went to press, our nation and world was stunned by the mass murder of school children in Newtown, Connecticut, a community not very far from where I live.

Those who 'believe in God,'[1] be they ordained minister or not, are thus forced to confront this question because people inevitably talk about it as they gather in their offices and other places of employment and converse about what is happening in the everyday lives of their communities and their world. Individuals less experienced in the life of organized religion or less inclined to come at life through the lens of a religious orientation often turn to those who 'believe' to hear their explanation of these seemingly senseless events: *It makes no sense that this innocent child was killed by a*

---

1 A phrase open to a variety of interpretations. Some, for example, see this as affirmation of a particular doctrine. Others approach it in terms of accepting a transcendent spiritual reality or force. These are but two of many approaches. It also requires that one ask an even deeper question: When one says one believes IN God, what are the characteristics and the activities of that God in whom one is placing one's faith?

drunken driver.' 'How can God allow these innocent, hungry children to endure even more famine and starvation? It's just not fair.'

One of the most popular 'religion' books on the market in the late twentieth century, a book which continues to sell large numbers of copies, deals with these very questions. In *When Bad Things Happen to Good People,*[1] Harold Kushner explores in detail these kinds of real life human questions with which we are confronted each day as he tells the intensely personal story of a tragedy that beset his own family and his detailed and thorough exploration of whatever possible meaning might lie behind it.

As I was considering a starting point for this sermon series and thus this book, I thought as well about the reality that there is an incredible amount of 'prayer language' out there in the world and that much of this language is spoken around issues of suffering. Thus both professional religious leaders (pastors, rabbis, imams, etc.) as well as those who are not are often asked to pray for someone. As a matter of fact, prayer intentions are often an integral part of regular worship services. In response to tragedy, both understandable and incomprehensible, it is not unusual for people to say or write words such as *'I will keep you (or him or her) in my prayers.'* These are often the very words used in mass marketed sympathy cards or other similar messages of condolence.

Within religious communities and contexts, the disclosure of suffering is often accompanied by the request for prayer. This is most certainly the case in the comment I cite below, the remark that formed the basis for the first and second messages in this series:

'Pastor Bob, will you pray for my wife? She's just been diagnosed with cancer and the prognosis doesn't look good. This just is not fair, Pastor!. She is such a good woman, has worked hard her entire life, and we were both really looking forward to her retirement so we could spend time together with our children and grandkids.'

---

1   See Harold Kushner, *When Bad Things Happen To Good People* (New York: Anchor Press, 1981).

How many times have we heard this kind of story and its accompanying request? It is a story that speaks of shattered dreams and the spiraling personal descent from contentment to hopelessness. It is so much a part of everyday living that, in my view, preachers and Christian teachers would be neglectful in ignoring the serious questions which it raises. This sad anecdote, one that I have heard all too often in my life and ministry, with genders and specifics varying within each situation, is the one that seemed most appropriate as a starting point for looking at the *real life* relationship between faith and everyday life.

In shaping the series however, I decided that this one quotation actually requires more than one sermon. In developing two messages and two separate conversations, I would thus be able to give adequate time to each of the separate, though intricately related, questions involved. As a result, the message I delivered which you will read in this chapter explores the suffering issue. The subsequent sermon and conversation (Chapter Two) delves into the nature, value and efficacy of prayer, including during those times when suffering has occurred.

Before you read this message and my commentary on our congregation's subsequent conversation, I want to examine how important it is to me that preachers and congregations confront together these questions about suffering within the context of a life oriented to both the existence and presence of God.

Of all the many religious questions a preacher has to address, is there a more important one than the relationship between the presence of God and the events that happen in peoples' lives, including the painful and tragic ones? As a clergyman, I have been very concerned over the years that these questions are often dealt with too glibly and with an air of spiritual certainty that denies the very complexity of the issue.

In response to the legitimate question of why people suffer, Christian believers have tended to resort to answers asserting that this suffering is *'part of God's plan,'* *'God's will for the person's life'* and with the accompanying assurance that *'things happen for a reason.'*

Through the history of the Christian faith, these ideas have developed first through a reading of ancient Biblical texts and secondly through the development of elaborate theological thinking around questions of the nature of God's will and God's omniscience, foreknowledge and even predestination of events and consequences.

In my view, it is the preacher's task to help her/his fellow worshiper, i.e. the one listening to the sermon, to sort through these complicated questions in light of both one's own personal life experience and sound factual information.

It is not antibiblical to claim that the worldview often expressed within the pages of scripture is representative of the knowledge base of a particular time in history. Without benefit of such scientific instruments as Doppler radar and the like, it is understandable why people might see a violent storm as an *act of God.'* It is not antireligious to claim that scientific knowledge can illumine our understanding of life and can pose new questions concerning faith.

Likewise, the Christian who holds to the conviction that God cares deeply about and loves each individual person and who strives in turn to respect those whom God has created might legitimately wonder why this loving God allows such terrible things to happen to those whom this divine Creator loves. A quick and easy doctrinally based answer *('God has a plan')* may not be enough to satisfy the impulses of this contemporary Christian's honest spirit.

As you will read in this chapter's sermon, as I was finishing up my work on this message, I received the tragic news that a fifteen year old girl from our local high school, a girl I knew and whose family I had worked with closely over the years, collapsed and died unexpectedly as she was preparing to do what she loved so much—perform onstage!

This kind of tragedy raises legitimate questions and deep consternation among those who are inclined to see life through the eyes of faith and, in my view, it is incumbent upon me, the preacher, to articulate and verbalize the disconnect between the simple assertions of faith and the reality of this terrible event e.g. if we believe God is so good, how can *'He'*[1] allow this to happen?

While there are those who would contend that it is the duty of the preacher to do what so many of Job's friends did and engage in a defense of their understanding of God,[2] I would suggest that it is in peeling away many of our suppositions that we are able to confront the enormity and the mystery of a God who is greater than our minds can ever imagine and whose mysteries cannot be labeled and simply placed in a box.

By raising legitimate questions and challenging suppositions about why God does what God does, the preacher both grants the hearer permission to express her/his own anger at injustice (a rather *'God like'* quality[3]) and to take a step in the direction of a faith tested in fire. By raising these questions, the preacher affirms that the Creator God endowed us with a mind with which to think and to confront both the contradictions of daily life and the unquestioned certainties upon which we have been raised. In doing so, the preacher also asserts what Rabbi Kushner does in his marvelous work–that God is very much present with us both in our seeking and in the consolation we receive as well as in the compassion we strive to express whenever senseless tragedy occurs.

In preaching this sermon, I hoped to spark some thought that might lead to conversation—perhaps in church that morning but, more importantly, in cars and offices, around water coolers and in family rooms as people moved out of church ... and into their week:

---

1   It is important, in my view, to be sure we do not limit our descriptions of God to masculine language, but rather seek a more expansive 'God talk.'
2   If you have not read these lengthy dialogues in the Book of Job in a while, I would suggest that they are worth a look!
3   There are numerous examples in the Gospels of Jesus' passion on behalf of the poor. See Matthew 25:31-46 as an important text in this regard.

WEEK ONE SERMON

EXCERPTS FROM JOB 1 AND 3, JOHN 9:1-12

'Pastor Bob, will you pray for my wife? She's just been diagnosed with cancer and the prognosis doesn't look good. This just is not fair, Pastor! She is such a good woman, has worked hard her entire life, and we were both really looking forward to her retirement so we could spend time together with our children and grandkids.'

This real life situation, I would imagine, reflects what many of us have heard in our lives all too many times ... We might hear it at work, or when someone calls us on the phone ... It is the kind of situation which is part of our 'Joys and Concerns' time here at church each week ... and nowadays, many of us might even become aware of this sort of sad occurrence when we log on to a Facebook page and watch its updated messages sit before us on our screens ...

When I think about this kind of request, *('Pastor, please pray for ... because this awful thing is happening')* I find that beneath the words there lies a plaintive cry — this sense that something is happening here in somebody's life and the life of those who love that somebody ... SOMETHING IS HAPPENING that is just not right or fair ... and there lies amidst these poignant words a cry of HOPE as well — that somehow, through this PRAYER, offered by this individual to whom I have entrusted my pain ... Through this PRAYER something good is going to happen, something better at least than this circumstance with which (in this example) this husband and wife are now confronted ... as they fear the loss of her life and HE FEARS the death of his precious companion ...

As I was finalizing this message, just two days ago, I, and many people I knew, were shocked by the sudden death of a 15 year old girl at the high school at which I work, a bright and happy young woman, who collapsed on stage doing one of the things in life she loved best — preparing to sing and dance in a performance scheduled to take place a few short hours later Friday night. I know her family well. My son Stephen performed on that same stage for years with her brother. I was counselor both for him and for her older sister and I was scheduled to be hers come this Fall. Her mom and dad are wonderful, kind and generous people and I have had the opportunity to get to know them throughout these last few years.

Over the course of these next few days … How many times will her parents and siblings hear the phrase 'I will pray for you' … ? They will get cards expressing sympathy, often signed off on with those words so often used when we can't think of any others … 'I will keep you in my thoughts and prayers' AND …

How many times will they wonder WHY? Why did this happen to our precious child? To the sister whom I loved? The very same question her friends wondered aloud as we gathered at our high school for a grief counseling session yesterday morning … And do you know what? An awful lot of people, both young and older … people who are promising 'thoughts and prayers' … THEY are wondering why as well … and it is NOT a bad thing that they are — because to see a parent's pain, to have before you the tears of the young, and to ask the question WHY — to be saddened by what seems so profoundly UNFAIR —

TO FEEL THAT WAY … is simply to be who we are created to BE — to feel the pain of those who suffer is to be what God created us to be — it is simply TO BE HUMAN … and to be human … even when it means we don't get it — TO SAY THAT WE DON"T KNOW WHY … to be human is good … it is very, very good! To be human, dare I say … and you will see why later — for us to be human, ISN'T THAT THE WILL OF GOD?

What we wonder about when bad things happen to the innocent is what drove the very writing of the Bible's classic Book of Job, excerpts of which we have read this morning … Chapter 1 describes (Job had everything … Then all gone …) … Chapter 3 lays out the questions and the depth of Job's pain — (why was I born?) … and the dialogue that follows lays out all the different approaches to this complex question — READ IT SOMETIME … seriously

... Over time, a variety of answers have emerged as explanations for awful things and unwittingly sometimes, we carry these answers around with us — you have heard these answers ... answers with which people comfort themselves and try to comfort one another.

> Everything happens for a reason
> It is all part of God's Will
> This was all predetermined

Back in the day, answers were constructed to explain all kinds of painful happenings, weren't they? And those answers have made their way down through the centuries ... But, then, for many people something happens inside when they witness something so blatantly unfair ... There is this inner disconnect they feel in their lives — this reality the experts call 'cognitive dissonance.'

What do I mean? ... Well ... we are taught ... and we pray ... and we sing ... about God's love ... and the blessings God has bestowed ... and then things happen that seem so blatantly unfair ... a girl in the prime of life collapses and dies, fires fill up the Colorado sky and put the houses and the lives of innocent people in jeopardy, a tornado kills little children in the Midwest, the poorest of the poor suffer from earthquakes, floods and a famine that will not go away ...

If I said to you ... list the injustices in life you know ... what a list we could construct, right? **And still the tapes play in our heads — Things happen for a reason — All part of God's will ... Part of the plan ...** With this kind of disconnect, this kind of cognitive dissonance, is it any wonder people might get angry at God?

Now, back in Jesus' day, people had their answers as well — Why was this young man born blind? EASY ANSWER — someone must have sinned to cause this to happen ... It was a simple, conventional answer BUT Jesus turned it upside down ... as HE INEVITABLY would always find a way to do ...

In 5 or 10 or 15 minutes, we are not going to answer the question 'why do bad things happen to the innocent' ... why this man's wife has to suffer from cancer or why other awful things happen as they do … … as a matter of fact, we are not even going to get to the PRAYER part of the question until Part Two in this series next week … But in 5 or 10 or 15 minutes, is it possible to both think and converse about the possibility that we, like Job's friends, have come up with a set of answers that limit our understanding of God and might even HURT IT?

Is it possible that in our attempt to explain why things happen, we are not being fair to God? That we are imposing limits on God? That WE, God's creatures, are PUTTING GOD IN A BOX?

Is it not possible when considering God to live with the MYSTERY that comes from being human? To make peace with the fact that God, by God's very definition, is greater than the greatest thoughts our mortal minds can conceive? And that ultimately God's LOVE is stronger and more powerful than all our love combined, yet, at the same time, the very source that gives us the power to LOVE, the very source for our capacity to fear the loss of someone dear, to witness the death of someone innocent, and shake our heads and say … 'It's just not fair …

THAT, DEAR FRIENDS … that COMPASSION, that SENSE OF JUSTICE, that feeling that THIS IS JUST NOT RIGHT … that comes from God as well … and let's not forget it …

All in God's will … all for a reason … Part of the plan …

AMEN!

LET'S TALK!

THE CONVERSATION

As I mentioned in our Introduction, this was not my church's first experience of discussing the sermon during the worship service. Yet, each time I do so, once the sermon is completed, I am left with a sense of uncertainty and wondering: *is anyone going to talk?* Now, theoretically, it is perfectly acceptable if no one talks. I really believe that the effect of a message might be very profound and deep as it is processed through a person's silence. I have also long been convinced that there is no value in the presence of wordiness, if its only purpose is to fill the air.

Nonetheless, when one pours some heart and soul into a message, one, at least THIS one writing these words, is hopeful that one will get some sense of how or if the message resonated with one's fellow travelers on this journey. And so, after the Amen, there was the wait. Within that wait there existed the possibility that these next few minutes would be filled by a lot of silence and more of me!

But then a thoughtful and sincere woman spoke, someone who has spoken often to me about what she has thought about during the week as she has reflected upon my Sunday sermon. She expressed how she could empathize with those who question and with Job's lament, as she too had experienced times that seemed all too dark. I could see from my perch in front of the congregation that she had hit a nerve as heads were nodding and attentiveness reigned. Somewhere along the line, she had made peace with the fact that there was more to life than living in despair. In scriptural terms, she opted to 'pick up her mat'[1] and walk.

Now, she did not say this but anyone who knows her would. Though she, by her own admission, had experienced intense pain and had been wounded, something has happened in her life and-consequently she has become a great source of consolation to all who know her- an example of kindness and mercy, a true role model for all of us who walk with her in our community called church.

This sense that we CAN know the presence of God through the presence and the actions of one another was verbalized in my congregation as well as people said that they KNEW God was present even amidst the terrible pain they were suffering. People spoke of others' *'being there'* for them in their times of need. What was interesting is that there was less concern that morning about GOD

1   See John 5:8

CAUSING tragedy and injustice and more with GOD ACTING through those who seek to alleviate it — e.g. it is more in keeping with faith to believe that God is present in the volunteer who provides help to victims in Haiti than that God caused the earthquake that made the victims suffer. This operative theology in real world living complements the insights offered by Rabbi Kushner in his marvelous book.

Another congregant recalled the minister in the days of his youth who reminded his church that we live here in a state of imperfection and that this is not heaven. He expressed contentment with the simple realization that the world as we know it is an incomplete and unfulfilled state. This led in to a woman's sincere expression that these questions must be so difficult for those who do not have faith.

At this point, I injected something which takes me back to my introductory words. I acknowledged that she definitely had a point and, as a person of faith, I know the consolation it brings me. BUT … I also contended that FAITH can also be a cause for discomfort and anger if the suppositions of faith do not connect with the totality of lived experience and human reason AND with other crucial aspects of faith.

In other words, our view of God CAN BE HURTFUL. Obviously, if we posit a whimsical, capricious God who can punish and predestine at will, for sure, but also if we have conjured up a God who CAN show mercy and CAN heal and alleviate pain and answer prayer with the desired result, yet for some godly reason, does not, how we perceive that God can impair our ability not only to comprehend but also to make peace in the midst of the current moment. One woman then wisely noted that it would not be unusual psychologically to project the anger that comes with uncertainty onto this being called God. I agreed with her noting that if you are going to get angry at big things, why not get angry at something (one) bigger than all, that is, God … ?

After worship, amazingly, even when I was not around, I was told that people were continuing the conversation and that, in essence, is what lies behind this approach to the preached Word which I have sought to describe. It is my hope then that as you end each chapter and consider the questions I will post that you and those around you will share in an ever deepened response to an ever present God who speaks to you, amidst and through the uncertainties of daily living …

DISCUSSION QUESTIONS

1. What is your understanding of God's will? Does God have a plan for your life? How do you know it?
2. How do you explain a 'good God' allowing the innocent to suffer?
3. Is faith helpful or harmful to you in facing tragedy? Explain by drawing on the experiences of your own life.
4. Can the human being 'know the mind' of God? If so, how?
5. Basic question: What does God do all day?

Chapter Two

In my second sermon in this series, I attempted to focus our examination on the same pastoral situation as the one we discussed in the first with a specific look at the different questions that might flow naturally from it. While our first message and conversation centered on the place of suffering in life and the issues surrounding God's will, this week's focus was the nature and the effectiveness of prayer. As the years have gone on in my ministry as a pastor and in my development as a person, I have become more acutely aware of the large number of built-in answers Christian believers have developed to respond to some of life's most troubling complexities and how important it is to hold those answers up to closer examination. Such, I have discovered, is definitely the case concerning the subject of prayer.

As I am writing these words, our nation is reeling from the horrific events that took place in Aurora, Colorado when during a midnight showing of the popular film *Batman,* an individual armed with a variety of weapons entered the theatre and proceeded to shoot and cause the death of a dozen human beings as well as the very serious and critical injuries of many others. In the aftermath of this horror, how many of us uttered the words that have been used over and over again in public: *'Let's keep the families of these victims in our thoughts and prayers.'?*

This phrase and others similar to it are typical responses we offer to others when we become aware of tragedies they or others are undergoing. In saying this, I am not being critical. for in uttering these words we are attempting to give shape and meaning and purpose in sad and troubling situations. Instead I am suggesting that it is important to seek clarification of the religious phraseology that we use. In my view, preachers and religious educators must be willing to raise these questions for in doing so they assist their congregations and their students in the process of delving more deeply and maturely into the mysteries of divine interaction with the world and with the creatures who inhabit it.

These pat responses which use religious language are everywhere. We see this clearly in the responses that are typical in dealing with the matter of God's will. We witness them in a variety of other areas as well: *'God needed another angel in heaven so He took her'* is a comment one hears quite often in religious circles, especially around the deaths of those who have suffered greatly or have been thought to die too young. Were we to stop and think about it, which I would encourage us to do, I think we would find a multiplicity of these set answers are part of peoples' knee jerk repertoire for times when words just don't come easy.

Now it needs to be clear that we are dealing with enormous mystery here and that our human intelligence and knowledge can only approximate the fullness of reality in the face of so many perplexing unknowns. Yet to the preacher, this is precisely the point. When I, as a clergyperson, am asked to pray for someone or when I lead a congregation in the weekly activity of praying for others, it is incumbent upon me that I consider and encourage others to examine seriously what it means to pray.

There are those who would contend that the very act of asking questions is threatening to the transmission of 'the faith.' They would argue that it is best to lead people toward finding clear and direct answers in the Bible. This 'proof texting' approach concerns me on a number of levels. First and foremost, it speaks to an incomplete view of scripture. Those who see the Bible as a book with set answers to complex questions miss the simple fact that the Bible portrays a people who, like us, are struggling with enormous mysteries (death, evil, sickness, etc.) and who respond to these mysteries both with profound questions and with a variety and a pluralism of answers.[1]

---

1   One of the most obvious examples is found in the accounts of the final hours of Jesus' own life when He raises serious questions during His own times of prayer.

In addition, this approach gives little respect to the reality that, for some reason, we human beings are gifted with intelligence and the ability to use our minds. Consequently, it strikes me that there is something healthy (maybe even in the divine grand design?) about using those minds to wonder and to doubt as well as to struggle with the many paradoxes life has a way of revealing.

My conviction on these issues leads me to try to craft sermons which lay the questions out there for all to see. In my view, this provides affirmation for those who harbor those questions and even honest doubts within themselves. Hearing them spoken can actually be quite liberating! In addition, I realize that many in a given congregation many never have really thought about or ever heard verbalized from a Christian preacher or teacher anything other than some prescribed set answer. While others would disagree with me, here is where I would contend that facing these questions and seeing beneath the surface are acts that can lead to an even deeper spirituality and faith than we might find when everything is approached simply on the surface.

Thus, in the sermon you will now read, I try to lay out the bottom line question: What difference does it make if you pray for someone? Underlying this is another important question: What does this prayer do? If one cuts even deeper one gets to an interesting contemporary take, that even if prayer does not have any effect upon God, does it still have effect upon the one praying and the one being prayed for?

Please note as you read this sermon that I do take the position that even with limited or no efficacy with regard to a 'result,' saying that one is praying for someone is an act of compassion and doing so in and of itself places one in contact with a depth that takes one far beyond the surface of ordinary existence. In other words, this very act does move one in the direction of that which Bonhoeffer has described as the 'beyond in our midst.'[1]

---

1   A well known phrase spoken by Dietrich Bonhoeffer, distinguished theologian, executed by the Nazis during World War Two.

Yet, having said that, I also encourage us not to stop there but to continue to open up the questions and thus to explore how we respond to how some of the answers actually depict God. In my scriptural selections for this sermon, I hold in juxtaposition the letter of James, part of the teaching on prayer from the Sermon on the Mount and Jesus' own moment in Gethsemane just a few hours before He died upon the cross.

James and the words from Jesus seem to make clear that prayer will have an effect. In James, praying for the sick can actually lead to healing. In the Gospel, persistence will pay off. However, I would also argue that there are two phrases we must consider which offer nuance to this position. In one, Jesus makes clear that the Father will not necessarily provide what the child wants but instead what he needs, thus qualifying the *'ask and you SHALL receive'* approach and that, in his own confrontation with death, Jesus recognizes that what happens is really out of His hands. Though I do not directly allude to it in the sermon, any conversation about these matters has to include the simple fact that, while hanging upon the cross, Jesus uttered the words of the 22nd Psalm (*'My God, My God, why have you abandoned [forsaken]) me?'*) thus presenting us with the clear reality that prayer is not limited to its desired effect but is also about internal struggle and conversation with the divine who lives both within and around us. There is precedent for this 'I-Thou,'[1] interpersonal, conversational approach throughout the Hebrew scriptures that were part of Jesus' very life. I cite the Book of Job and many of the Psalms as rather clear examples.

As you will see when we look at the conversation that followed this message, the congregation in my church that morning was willing to give this topic considerable thought. I would contend that they would do so because it is so real. Tragedy is part of life. People tend to want what is best for their world and for those whom they love. We also live enshrouded by mystery. We see dimly and don't get the whole picture.[2] On some level, many of us realize that

1   A phrase coined by the Jewish scholar Martin Buber.

2   See I Corinthians 13

the answers we have been given are not completely satisfactory, not because they are the wrong answers, but simply because they take great complex questions and simplify them to the point where, in moments of our honesty with ourselves, they can be so readily refuted.

As you read this sermon, I invite you to examine your reaction to the questions that I pose and, as you read about our conversation, I also encourage you to find a way to join it as well.

WEEK TWO SERMON

JAMES 5:13-18, LUKE 11:1-13

'Pastor Bob, will you pray for my wife? She's just been diagnosed with cancer and the prognosis doesn't look good. This just is not fair, Pastor!. She is such a good woman, has worked hard her entire life, and we were both really looking forward to her retirement so we could spend time together with our children and grandkids'

'Pastor Bob, will you pray for my wife?
'I will pray for you'
'Let's keep each other in our prayers'

As a pastor, I get a lot of requests from people — sometimes they ask that I pray for them. Other times they request that I pray for someone close to them. My best guess is that you promise YOUR prayers to other people as well ... to relatives, friends, those with whom you work, or used to work ... My sense is that we all feel that by offering to pray, we are DOING SOMETHING when the circumstances leading us to prayer are so awful and so out of our hands ... when words fail us and seem so limiting ... Speaking personally, when I hear someone say 'My wife has cancer' or when I attend or officiate at the funeral of a child ... there is a certain POWERLESSNESS that I feel and so ... offering to pray is a way of breaking through that loss of control ... by taking some kind of action, right?

When feeling helpless, it's a way of feeling that you are helping ... and I trust, in fact, that you are ... Yet, you see, underlying any request for prayer or any promise of prayer, I think, there lies this often unspoken question of prayer's EFFECT — If I promise that man, I will pray for his wife, will it make any difference in how his wife feels or whether she is cured? Will praying for the parents of the teenager I know who died suddenly ... will praying FOR THEM bring them any PEACE? ANY CONSOLATION? Will it bring them any closer to healing and going on with their lives?

At some point, the Christian who comes to church has to come face to face with the question — what does prayer DO? You see, we know that promising prayer can be a consoling act of kindness — '*You are in my thoughts and prayers*' ... 'PRAYER' such a kind word that I saw someone use it recently by saying to me that' We will send you our thoughts and our prayers,' causing me to think ... 'But, don't we send our prayers to God?' (Don't mind me — sometimes I just get hyper theological!)

We also know that the ACT OF PRAYER-the act itself — of quiet time, of meditating (as some people do), of getting away from the mad rush of daily life — THE VERY ACT can be comforting and stress relieving ... Yet, knowing all of this still begs the question — WHAT DOES PRAYER DO? If I pray for the poor and hungry, what does that do about poverty and hunger? If I pray for peace, does that stop war? PUT FANCIFULLY — One of the great questions believers must face is less than a simple one — What is the EFFICACY of prayer? ... In other words, what is its effect ... or, more appropriately, is there a CAUSE and EFFECT relationship between praying ... and something happening?

Pretty big questions, huh?

If we look at today's Scripture passages, we get the strong sense that back in Bible days ... YEAH, there was this relationship, this causal connection. — Elijah prayed for rain. It rained ... The church will pray for healing ... so people will get healed, James seems to imply ('The prayer of faith will save the sick') ... Jesus says 'ask and you will receive ... be persistent and knock and the door will be opened to you.'

But then the Bible gives us another side of this as well — Jesus sweats drops of blood in the garden — begging not to die — but then He just up and says — to God — 'Not my will but yours ... '-and then the next day HE DIES — And, in less than a throwaway line right after this 'ask and receive' sequence ... you get this interesting comment from Jesus that God 'The Father' is going to end up giving His child what He needs, throwing the door open to the possibility that not everything we want and ask for is what we need, right?

So, again, we have this **depth** in the Bible that is not readily apparent to those who just toss out verses to prove their point ... Side note — that REALLY is a pet peeve of mine — when people just throw Bible passages at you out of context ...

Happened to me Friday morning on a beach — I was talking to someone who had read my book and while she disagreed with some of what I wrote there, she was making her points to me both respectfully and intelligently ... And then this woman, from a few feet away, someone whom I had never met before, began challenging my answers ... at one point calling out: 'What about I Corinthians 11?? '

Now ... tell me ... do you think I backed off and resisted this conversation? NO ...

But, my point here is not that — Just as that woman had that passage from the Bible way out of context and was actually saying it was talking about things it wasn't even going anywhere near talking about, we have to be careful with how we use the Bible ... We've got to get the big picture behind each little verse — The stakes are too high not to do so! ...

At any rate, this morning, before we break into conversation, I want to place before you a few ideas ... for us to think about ... and perhaps discuss here ... or at home ... or preferably both ...

It is good to tell others we will pray for them.

By saying we will pray, we show that we care.

In the very act of praying, we connect ourselves with God ... We go to a place inside of us that transcends 'the world' as we know it ... We step into the 'God life,' a life which undergirds and sustains daily life, but a life so easy to disregard and ignore ... You see, God is the most real REALITY we can ever know ... the very ground of our very being ...

And since God is LOVE and COMPASSION — when I tell that man that I will pray for his wife with cancer and that I will pray for him as well, when I tell the grieving parent she is in my prayers, when I pray at the bedside of one who is about to pass over from this life to the next, when you say that you will keep that person in YOUR PRAYERS, **we** are deeply engaging in the action of God who, after all, is what? ... What does the Bible say? God IS LOVE, correct?

And when we pray, it is OK to ask God questions — 'How can this be, O God? How can this terrible thing be happening?'

It is good to be honest — 'God, I don't understand.'

It is not even bad to offer God suggestions — 'Would you consider healing this person, please?'

Nor is it 'unholy' to even throw some frustration or anger at God ... 'God, this isn't fair! This little child did NOTHING to deserve this!'

BUT ... and this is MOST IMPORTANT — what is significant in ALL of these actions I have just described is that it is what you have got going between you and God that really counts ... It is this thing called a RELATIONSHIP — Dare I say that WE WERE CREATED in order to relate to God? The great philosopher Martin Buber described this beautifully as an 'I- Thou' relationship —

You see, prayer is not about doing things just right or often enough so that in doing so, you get God to do what you want (Protestants, with their Reformation rebellion against works righteousness should be the last to think that!)

NO — WHEN PUSH COMES TO SHOVE AND WHEN THE RUBBER HITS THE ROAD-PRAYER is about LIVING WITH, TALKING TO, STANDING OR SITTING IN AWE OF … the greatest MYSTERY one can ever imagine — the mystery that is responsible ULTIMATELY for the YOU WHO IS YOU … as well as the one for whom YOU ARE PRAYING …

WE ARE TALKING ULTIMATELY, DEAR FRIENDS, ABOUT THE ULTIMATE MYSTERY … THE MYSTERY THAT IS GOD!

And so, then, let us pray … in song:

Day by day, day by day, oh, dear Lord, three things I pray: To see thee more clearly, love thee more dearly, follow thee more nearly, day by day (Repeat several times)
AMEN

THE CONVERSATION

Over the course of my years as a pastor, as I have mentioned, I have encouraged dialogue about my message on many occasions. Inevitably, at the conclusion of each message, I have found that I experience a period of uncertainty as I wait to see if anyone will talk or whether we will all move on together to the next part of the service. While I strongly believe, as I have articulated to my congregation and stated in our previous chapter, that even were no one to speak there would be value in this period of shared reflection, I will admit that during this time, I wait in hope that someone will start a conversation.

Interestingly enough, upon the completion of this particular message, people really had a lot to say once they got rolling and they did so with a lot of conviction. From those who spoke, there was really a consensus that the very act of praying for someone is a good thing in and of itself. There was far less advocacy for the position that prayer persuades God than for the belief that one is doing a good thing spiritually *for oneself and for someone else* by extending the offer of prayer.

This is not to say that people denied prayer's efficacy as a couple of individuals made clear that prayer has made a specific difference at critical times in their lives and they cited powerful examples. Instead it is to point out that, even where certainly does not exist on the cause and effect relationship of prayer, members of my congregation, including their pastor, indicated that they felt uplifted and connected to something greater when they both prayed for someone and were the recipient of a promise of prayer.

In my own response to one individual, I reflected upon my reaction to the massive outpouring of support for me during the time of my recent surgery and subsequent recovery period. To be perfectly honest, while I had most assuredly appreciated the cards, emails, texts and scrumptious food deliveries as they were occurring, it was in the context of this conversation where I was struck even more deeply than I was during the time when I was undergoing and rehabilitating from relatively minor hip replacement surgery.

Parenthetically, my reaction is indicative of a potentially good outcome in this preaching/conversation process. The reflective conversation within the community impacted the depth of my reflection. I have seen this over and over again in retreat settings, especially among youth, and I strongly believe that it is a workable model for occasional use within the congregational worship context.

While this one period of reflection can never be held up as providing all necessary data to consider the power and value of prayer, I do believe our conversation indicates some current trends in theological thinking that exists among mainstream believers. There was no overt movement within the congregation either to affirm the direct relationship between prayer and outcome or to deny its possibility. Instead the focus reflected a more contemporary understanding of the relational aspects of supporting one another, in this case through giving and receiving the promise of prayer.

This, in my view, is indicative of a certain pragmatic approach to religious faith that exists within our culture. On the other hand, it cannot be easily dismissed as a Norman Vincent Peale like 'power of positive thinking'[1] approach which can readily lapse into a utilitarian approach to the practice of religion. Underlying our conversation was the deeper conviction that there is a spiritual connectedness to others AND to the divine within any act of prayer. In my view, this in itself is indicative of prayer's profound spiritual value, even were one to remain uncertain on the specific question of its actual effect.

As we wrapped up our second week in this series, I was most pleased that in exploring these complex and interrelated questions of the nature of God's will and the place of prayer in the overall human/divine dialectic, our congregation was both witnessing to and teaching one another as we sought to continue to grow in our relationship with the very source of our lives, the very object of our faith!

DISCUSSION QUESTIONS

1. In your view, can prayer have any effect upon what God does?
2. Can prayer help someone be healed? Explain your answer.
3. Even if prayer would not affect the outcome, is there a value in prayer?
4. What is the distinction between prayer and superstition?
5. Have you ever benefited from someone praying FOR YOU? Explain.

---

1 Norman Vincent Peale popularized this approach and had an impact on other Christian preachers, most notably Rev. Robert Schuller

CHAPTER THREE

As I was driving home from church on one recent Sunday morning, I happened upon a radio interview with Dr. Thomas Groome, a distinguished Roman Catholic religious educator. In the interview, he was discussing his recent book so aptly entitled *Will There Be Faith?*[1] In this work, which I rushed off to purchase soon after I heard this interview, Groome articulates the concern, held by many within the Christian community, that those young people initiated and educated in a religious tradition are not necessarily likely to 'practice that faith'[2] when they move into adulthood.

Quite honestly, I went into the reading of Groome's book expecting that he would be focused on the Roman Catholic community. One could not fault him were that the case because he is a distinguished catechetical leader within it. As I moved through its pages, I was pleasantly surprised that his message, while most helpful to Roman Catholics, had a broader applicability. As a matter of fact, as a mainline Protestant Christian who believes firmly in the 'ecumenical center' we share with the Catholic faith,[3] I was most pleased with how Groome addressed issues that ought to be of common concern.

Interestingly enough, on the day upon which I listened to this radio interview, I was already in the process of developing the sermon which you will find later on in this chapter. The inspiration for this next message in the series was the many questions I have received from parents about both the process of transmitting Christian faith to their children and their profound concerns that Christian faith will not mean as much to these children in their adult years as it does to those parents today.

---

1   See Thomas Groome, *Will There Be Faith?*(New York: Harper One, 2011).

2   A popular phrase for being active in a particular faith tradition.

3   I explore this in detail in my book *Crossing the Street*.

Coupled with this worry is the sense that the institutional church itself is in some kind of trouble. While Groome acknowledges this problem within his own community of faith, it is quite clear that it is not limited to Roman Catholics. Major declines in church attendance and denominational loyalty have been well documented for years within mainline Protestant church bodies. In my native New England, several Congregational churches with deep roots in the history of the region's towns have closed their doors. Well known crises have troubled church bodies that have been well established for generations.

When I was a Roman Catholic Permanent Deacon working in a suburban parish, I was struck by the small number of weddings that took place in that church each year. The problem, as I saw it, was that a large number of young people seemed disconnected from that community. It may have been the place where they trained for and received the sacraments, but it was not a place with which they felt a strong emotional and spiritual bond. My experience as a Protestant clergyperson has taught me that this situation is most assuredly not limited to Catholicism alone.

Lest one assume a doomsday posture with respect to this behavior, it should also be noted that in situations in which a person marries someone from another religious tradition, finding a place to marry which does not simply reflect one of the partner's upbringings, is both a sensitive and sensible approach. In addition, many couples are more 'tuned in' to recognizing the presence of the divine in settings outside of the church building (e.g. beach, lake, mountain, etc.) than may have been the case a generation or more ago. I have officiated or been present at many deeply religious ceremonies of matrimonial commitment held outside the walls of a church building.

As I prepared the sermon you are about to read, I had these factors and issues all weighing upon my mind:

1. The legitimate concerns of people I know that the institution of the church, especially the mainline church, might be in deep trouble as we face the future.

2. The IMPORTANCE of a healthy mainstream Christianity as a real alternative to the growing phenomenon of evangelical/ fundamentalist churches, often of the independent or megachurch variety.

3. The reality that because institutional church loyalty may be down, it does not necessarily follow that spirituality is on the decline.[1]

4. The conviction, which Groome argues so well in his groundbreaking book, that when all is said and done, the future of faith depends upon helping young people (and older ones among us too) to focus upon Jesus. This is coupled with my conviction that, all too often, the church is seen as a social institution or as part of who a particular group is as a culture and NOT seen enough as a community of individuals (from a variety of cultural contexts) who seek to be faithful disciples of Jesus and who take His teachings with utmost seriousness!

As you read this sermon and my commentary about the subsequent conversation that we held, I ask that you examine your thoughts and feelings with respect to what I have just expressed. I am hopeful that the discussion questions I provide at the end of this chapter will be useful in this regard.

WEEK THREE SERMON

DEUTERONOMY 4:1-9; 20-25, LUKE 2:41-52, LUKE 18:8

'You know, Pastor, I am really worried about the future of the church. My 16 year old son has absolutely no interest in attending and I see such a difference between the world in which he is growing up and what it was like back when I was his age. Sometimes I wonder if the importance of religion is going to fade away'

---

1   See Lillian Daniel, *'When 'Spiritual But Not Religious' Is Not Enough.* (New York: Jericho Books,2013). She has some unique and thought provoking takes on this issue. Worth a serious read.

Today's message and conversation takes place with the back-drop of those haunting words we just heard from the 18th chapter of Luke where Jesus wonders aloud: *'When the Son of Man comes, will He find faith upon the earth?'* And these words which I have just cited from a parent reflect pretty accurately some of the real life changes we know we have experienced over the course of our lifetimes.

In short, it is a pretty accurate statement of the way things really are. Allow me to use myself as an example: I am a baby boom baby, born just a few years after my father got home from World War II. Back when I was young, churches were crowded on Sunday mornings — Catholic, Protestant — they were well attended. Of course, there were people who did not go to church and we don't want to paint a rosy, fantasy like picture — but the SOCIAL NORM was that going to church is what one does on Sunday and the accompanying expectation was that this norm would continue as young church people became adults.

But, if we fast forward to 2012, we see a different picture — The rosiest spin we can put on the numbers indicates that at most 30% of those who claim to be affiliated with a church attend on any given Sunday. There have been major increases in the number of people who have no church connection AND, in many denominations, there has been a significant dropoff in the number of young people who participate in the activities of their local churches, much less attend Sunday worship …

So, then, the adult speaking these words IS ONTO SOME-THING. Yes, when it comes to religion, even if we shave away the tendency to see the grass as so much greener than — # 1 We ARE living in a different world and # 2 — This all DOES raise signifi-cant questions about the future of the church …

But, my friends, this morning, before we break into conversa-tion, I would like to draw some distinctions. And I would like to do that by suggesting that we really are dealing with three uniquely different questions — in looking at these questions about religion and the future. … In doing so, I would like to suggest that the

traditional norms are not the only way to examine the big picture
—

What do I mean? Well, let's start with this — Even if tradition-al indicators are down — if people are not going to church as they did in the early 60's and kids are not beating down the doors to get into youth programs — does that necessarily mean that SPIRITU-ALITY is dying, that is, the quest to discover meaning and purpose and value in life? I would like to suggest that this awareness that there is more to life than meets the eye, that a conversation about God is a valuable one to have — is still there — It is there in our young people and it's there in a large number of everyday adults for whom church attendance has not become a habit of their lives ...

Secondly, while one would think that attending church would lead one to a deeper interest in Jesus, perhaps we need to admit that, for a lot of people churches project more an image of a club or or-ganization that 'does things,' albeit good things, than a community on fire with the words and teachings of Jesus —

All of which inevitably leads us back finally to what is ex-pressed in these words from a congregant to a pastor — will church be part of the life of this young generation as they take their place as adults or will the numbers continue to dwindle and will church as we know it fade away? I would be less than truthful if I did not acknowledge that there ARE church communities in which many young people are actively involved AND which do place a heavy emphasis on personal faith in Jesus ...

UNFORTUNATELY ... and some would really quarrel with me here ... most of these churches don't fall under the umbrella of 'mainline' American religion — For the most part, numbers are down among Catholics, Episcopalians, Methodists, UCC, Luther-ans, Orthodox and among their youth — down within the same churches that were flourishing back in the baby boom years, the heyday of American institutional religion

Where you will see these increases are in the megachurches, the independent churches, the new church starts that have popped up in many communities — Now I said UNFORTUNATELY and I said that people will quarrel with me and here is why they will — Some would argue that these churches are getting the word of God out to those who need to hear it-and that they are 'saving souls.' How can you argue with that?

I won't, except to say that I am concerned that many of these churches present young people (and us older ones too) a view of Christianity that both pits faith against reason (It's bad to believe in evolution) and employs a selective literal interpretation of the Bible, often coupled with an extremely rigid understanding of marriage, family, and human sexuality.

I will also say that for many of these churches the emphasis is more on 'accepting Jesus' and less on really delving into HOW Jesus wants us to live — putting the Sermon on the Mount center stage for example in the way that we shape our moral living.

I will end with yet another summertime anecdote from the beach — As this woman of whom I spoke last week was challenging me regarding my interpretation of church law and Communion based on I Corinthians 11, there I was sitting near a young adult post baby boom couple ... This couple looked upon this conversation as if they were watching a foreign film with subtitles ... for the old language of church and law and rules was not really relevant to their lives ...

I want to suggest that the point of connection for them, as well as for the mainline churches of the future, IS a renewal of intense and serious examination of who Jesus is and what He taught. In short, churches have really got to get serious and passionate about JESUS!

For, in Jesus, I would contend, one will find an answer to one's innate spiritual longings and in the mission of Jesus, one would find a REASON FOR BEING PART OF THE CHURCH!

Let's talk ...

THE CONVERSATION

When this sermon ended, I opened up the floor for observations and questions. Immediately, an older member of my congregation, someone for whom our church was so integral a part of his life, rose and asked me a question he had raised with me before: '*Why*, he asked, *are these other churches so successful in getting new members and growing?*'

Of course, beneath the surface of that question, lies some hard and cold reality. There were churches in our little area of New England, which happened not to be members of the United Church of Christ, which have added a lot of members over the years, even to the point where they have had to expand their facilities. At the same time, other churches in nearby communities had struggled, some even facing the reality of actually closing. The man definitely had a pretty solid observation. If you are looking at church growth, attendance, numbers of members, additions of facilities and even staff, these churches are quite successful indeed.

The answer I gave is one that I had given before, one which I believe quite strongly and an answer that I am most aware some others might contest. I believe that many of these churches work very hard at creating a view of the world for would-be congregants which is a real alternative to that which they experience out in the world every day.[1] They are extremely successful in providing activities that are well organized for children, teenagers, families and those going through the difficulties life can throw at you. I alluded to the fact that when our children were young, my wife used to attend a Bible Study at a conservative church in our town. This program was deliberately geared for young mothers whose children spent a lot of time with them at home.

The technical excellence of many of these programs, I said, is definitely worth applauding. My area of contention lies with my belief that some of these churches use these outreach programs to

---

1   See my exploration of this in Robert R. LaRochelle, *Part Time Pastor, Full Time Church* (Cleveland, Pilgrim Press, 2010).

create an alternative universe with regard to Christian faith, an approach which I find is quite lacking in many ways. Now it is important to note, and I pointed this out as part of my response, that Christianity IS an alternative to the 'ways of the world,' for sure. Yet the specifics of what that alternative should be, in my view, is a problem with this evangelical/fundamentalist/conservative vision of Christianity.

In these churches, what is taught in public schools is suspicious. In the views of many of their leaders and members, public schools are places where tolerance of homosexuality is espoused, where one cannot pray and one is expected not to evangelize on behalf of one's own religious conviction. Public schools are places which are 'soft on evolution' and where you will not find teaching according to the view of Biblical inerrancy these churches see as essential to real Biblical faith.

I explained to my congregation that, in practical terms, these congregations and their pastors hold to a literal interpretation of the Biblical principle of tithing. In this view, it is normal and expected that one would give 10% of one's income to the church. In pragmatic terms, there is an awful lot that a church can do with 10% of its members' incomes. I explained that 'mainline' churches are disinclined to view the principle of tithing as a legal stipulation and to see giving in broader terms.

Beyond that, though, I pointed out that, in my opinion, many of these 'successful' churches have presented a view of Christianity which poses an insufficient acknowledgment of the importance of the use of reason and of science. In my view, I said, they oversimplify some of the toughest questions of faith.

Much of the response from the congregation that morning centered on their perceptions that some of the 'non mainstream' churches were more focused on the idea of raising money. One particular individual who had recently started attending our church indicated that he was very turned off by the approach he found in some of the other local churches he had tried out. The primary reason he did not proceed to pursue attendance or membership there was this emphasis on finances. Others shared similar concerns.

In my response, I noted that it would be unfair to categorize all such churches as focused on financial giving. In their defense, I noted, many of them do really outstanding ministerial work. While there certainly is precedent for abuse in organized religion, the reality is that the extreme examples are exactly that- extreme! The greater concern I have is that I believe organized Christianity is in danger of losing churches and adherents whose focus is more along the lines of what has ordinarily been described as mainline Christianity. In many circles, this approach is known nowadays as progressive or liberal Christianity.

I tend to be a bit wary of these titles that are so readily tossed around in political parlance. There is a divisiveness in American political conversation that I would like to see the church transcend. So, even as I am most comfortable calling myself progressive, I see mainline Christianity as being an approach which respects the various perspectives individual Christians may have on the kinds of issues which are of concern to believers. I think the church needs local communities where people are able to remain in dialogue with one another, even if they differ in their approach to any number of issues.

While, in our discussion, I tried to emphasize the importance of bolstering churches such as the one which I pastor, I do not believe that this work can be done in the period of one sermon and one conversation. I do believe however that it is among the most important work to be done in American Christianity over these next several decades. Though I appreciated the fact that the congregation gathered on that July morning in our small sanctuary valued and cherished the work of our little church, I believe it is an area that must be spoken about and given high priority now and in the foreseeable future. Many churches are closing — and I find this sad and, in a lot of cases, absolutely short sighted and unnecessary. There is uncharted territory in the area of new church starts, territory that must continue to be explored.[1]

As we discussed that morning, it is really important that children and emerging adolescents have the opportunity to engage in serious religious conversation during their formative years. I believe that the mainline church must work very hard to be sure not to yield the area of Christian Education to the church's more fundamentalist elements. I was grateful for the comments that were made by those in our congregation that morning who were familiar with the approach we take toward the formation of our youth. Intensive focus on Christian Education and Youth Ministry on the parish level and Campus Ministry on the collegiate are crucial if we seek to 'transmit' the Christian faith in a way that has an impact years down the road and which answers positively the question Thomas Groome so succinctly asks: *'Will there be faith?'*

DISCUSSION QUESTIONS

1. What is your level of concern for 'the future of faith'? Are you pessimistic? Optimistic? Explain.
2. What is your opinion of the author's critique of conservative/evangelical/fundamentalist Christianity?
3. What can organized Christianity (the church) do better in reaching out to young people?
4. What examples can you give of spiritual themes found in film, television, or music? Explain.
5. What do you think of the author's emphasis on the teachings of Jesus as the focal point for Christian formation? How can that be done more effectively in your church, denomination or particular context?

---

1 I commend *The Center for Progressive Renewal* for their outstanding, groundbreaking work in this area.

Chapter Four

In our first two sermons and conversations, we explored in some depth the question of what God DOES with respect to responding to what is happening within our personal lives and in the wider world. We looked at questions of suffering and examined, among other things, the cause and effect dynamics involved in the act of prayer. In our third week, we took a break from these questions about God and moved into some specifics involving the very future of the Christian faith which we espouse. In this, our fourth week, we returned to some very basic and fundamental questions about God, questions that, in my view, need to be addressed directly and regularly if we wish to continue to grow in our faith.

Whereas the earlier message concentrated on the issue of God's ACTIVITY in our world, this sermon cuts even deeper as it explores the very issue of WHO or WHAT God is. Of course, if one posits the concept that God is a WHO, this notion of the 'personal God' begs even more questions. One might wonder about how God looks or whether God possesses the characteristics which we associate with 'person.'

In honesty, the idea of God as person has dominated much of the popular 'God talk' down through the years and is found in the language and the imagery used to describe God in traditional Sunday school and catechism parlance. The contravening concept of God as Spirit or 'ground of being' is often hard for people to grasp. as walking down the road of that particular theological approach might bring one close to declaring an impersonal concept of God which might not seem entirely adequate.[1]

What I attempt to do in this sermon is to put all of the core questions regarding God's essence out on the table for people to consider. Believing as I do that in the homiletic context, it is not <u>enough to simply</u> toss out the questions, I invite the hearers to

1   This is the danger of an impersonal 'theism.'

consider the reality that our very inability to describe God is, in fact, a testimony to the power and the awesomeness of God. Along these lines, I decry the ways that our understanding of God has been limited and how we have found multiple ways to define and describe God in the narrowest of terms. As a noted thinker once pointed out: *'God created human beings in God's image and we human beings have proceeded to return the favor.'*[1]

As you explore this sermon, I encourage you to take the time to consider your own responses to these questions I put before the congregation and before you. In addition, as you read about the subsequent conversation, I ask you to think about what YOU might have said if you were in one of those pews on that hot summer morning reflecting upon these questions I put before you.

WEEK FOUR SERMON

PSALM 46:1, PSALM 139, EXODUS 3:13-14, I JOHN 4:13

' Pastor Bob, tell me about God. What do we really know about God? What's God really like? Where is God? When I pray, does God hear? Is God telling me things? Is God like a person ... or more like an idea?'

These simple, yet complicated, questions, spoken by a young person at a church retreat, are extremely interesting and informative- AND for several reasons-First of all, there is this underlying assumption, I think, that, as a minister, I can really answer them, just as I can somehow explain or defend why the suffering of the innocent takes place, why God could create a world where someone could just walk into a movie theatre and embark on a massive killing spree ... You see, people turn to certain people to explain that which is unexplainable, even when the people asked wonder about the same things as do those doing the asking ...

---

1   This has been attributed to George Bernard Shaw.

AND ... Secondly, this question points to the fact that, in reality, even if any of us considers oneself a 'person of faith,' we have to admit, when faced with all of the complexities of life's questions, that there really is a lot that we DON'T KNOW about God-That even if we know our Bibles well, there is so much about God that we cannot explain, that those Bibles themselves contain hundreds of images and descriptions of God, many of them different from some of the others ...

Now, there are those who would argue vociferously with me and say that I am wrong – that God is completely known and all that I have to do is just believe it ... And there are those throughout history who have spoken with absolute certainty about God's intentions — To them, there is NO DOUBT, for example, that the way they see God is the one and only way.

For them, what others might call terrorism or hatred is really God's will!

They are very comfortable telling you exactly what God is thinking ... and for them there is wonderful comfort in how God, in their minds, just happens to give divine voice to the prejudices and fears they harbor within and that God will justify and endorse whatever they choose to do, all in God's name ...

You take bias, hatred, prejudice and fear and you put God in the mix — and the unthinkable starts sounding downright holy — and this crosses over cultures and religions, dear friends — I am not just talking about terrorists driving planes into buildings ...

So, you see these questions from this young person — What can you tell me about God? What's God really like? — they beg all kinds of other questions — questions we have examined in weeks before — How does God deal with our prayers? Why do such terrible things happen ... and are allowed by God? What is God's will?

Now, not everyone walks through everyday life spending a lot of time thinking (much less talking) about these questions ... a lot of us are much more practical and spend our time thinking about our jobs and our loved ones and paying the bills ... BUT ... whether we are inclined to go deep and philosophical or just take life day to day, we really DO walk through our lives with concepts and images of God floating around in our heads and INFLUENC-ING the way that we act ...

I remember being with a friend of mine, who is a Catholic, and it was a Friday in Lent when he realized that, by mistake, un-intentionally, he had eaten a slice of pizza with meat on it ... He was upset with himself and said that he had broken the law — I told him not to worry about it and then asked, rather flippantly, if he really thought that with everything going on in the world, God had time to punish people for biting into a slice of pepperoni?

Now, don't misunderstand me ... I think there is great value in the Catholic tradition of Lenten sacrifice — that's not my point ... Instead, what I am saying is this ... Behind many of the ways in which people approach the practice of religion (Protestant, Catho-lic, Jew, Muslim, any religion ...) , there lies this image of God ... and what God expects from us, an image which may not always jive with who God really is ... but which becomes to the practitioners of that religion, the way things are meant to be ...

So, then back to the question, when you think of God, what do YOU think about? Do you see God as a person? Does God have feelings? Or is God more like a spirit, a spirit who is always around, but whose characteristics are not the same as us mere mortals?

One of the great insights about God ever written was that of the distinguished Jewish philosopher Martin Buber who said that when we think of this reality called God — we have got to look at it in terms of a RELATIONSHIP, a personal relationship between the I and Thou, the I and You, that is yourself, myself ... and God ... A RELATIONSHIP!!!

You see ... God has often been viewed historically as a law giv-er and a judge, even as one who has predetermined our fate before we were ever born, but Buber said that the essence, the heart and soul of religion, is this relationship between I and person and the Thou that is God —

That is the crux of Psalm 139, isn't it, the Psalm we just read ... 'Lord, you have searched me and you know me ... 'the relationship of I and Thou ... Yet, even with that, which I think is so profoundly true and was so much a part of Jesus too (Abba, Father, Daddy) — is it not still possible that we LIMIT God by thinking only in human categories and by means of human language?

Is it not possible that NO WORDS can ever describe God because a. God is beyond words and human language and b. our human minds simply cannot grasp God — ??

AND, think about this ... isn't it possible that REAL WORSHIP , worship in spirit and in truth, is built upon the reality that we SIMPLY DO NOT UNDERSTAND?? — *'Immortal, invisible, God only wise, in light inaccessible hid from our eyes ... ,'* the hymn reminds us!

A FINAL THOUGHT FOR CONSIDERATION — Christian faith, as it has developed down through the centuries, has spoken of God as Father, Son and Holy Spirit — This language itself suggests that God cannot be easily pinned down and limited, right? (Three 'persons' in one God??)

Anyway, this notion of Trinity is often taught as some fact of faith that people just recite rather rotely when they sing the Doxology or verbalize what they believe ... What I would like to suggest is that if you look at the ACTIVITY expressed in this Trinitarian formula — you are really getting to the heart of this God to whom we can relate day in and day out ...

You see, this God is our CREATOR, our REDEEMER and our SANCTIFIER — those are the activities of Father, Son and Spirit — and, right here and right now, in the very moments of each and every life, God is working to create us, to free us and to bring us closer and deeper into relationship with the divine ... God, who once created, continues to create NOW — (Ps 51- create in me a clean heart, O God),[1] God who redeemed us in Jesus, offers redemption every moment we live, and God who once sent the Holy Spirit, is present in that spirit today, present in our hearts, present in EACH OTHER ...

---

1   Psalm 51:1

While this side of paradise, we cannot know and understand everything — and so much so necessarily- is well beyond our grasp, and while we may not know every answer to exactly how or why or when or if God does certain things, can we still not believe that, well beyond the limitations of our minds, there is a God, a God who, just as certainly, dwells right here within us ... ??

LET US PRAY:

MY LORD GOD, I have no idea where I am going. I do not see the road ahead of me. I cannot know for certain where it will end. Nor do I really know myself, and the fact that I think I am following your will does not mean that I am actually doing so. But I believe that the desire to please you does in fact please you. And I hope I have that desire in all that I am doing. I hope that I will never do anything apart from that desire. And I know that if I do this you will lead me by the right road, though I may know nothing about it. Therefore I will trust you always though I may seem to be lost and in the shadow of death. I will not fear, for you are ever with me, and you will never leave me to face my perils alone.
AMEN[1]

THE CONVERSATION

At the end of this message, once again, there was a period of deep silence. For a moment, I wondered if anyone in that church was going to say anything. This happened more than once in the course of this series' first few weeks! Of course, my premise, in presenting this kind of series is that even if no one speaks, there remains a value in offering the opportunity. In fact, the questions raised from a pulpit on a Sunday should never just be confined to that day. Ideally, I am hopeful that people might talk about them in those many and varied places in which they live out their daily lives.

---

1 This prayer was written by the renowned Trappist monk, Thomas Merton.

It was not long though before someone shared something with all of us gathered on that warm, sultry New England Sunday, the most humid Sunday of this rather steamy summer. Of all of the concepts I laid out there for people to explore, the one that reso-nated the most was that this God of ours knows us and really does care! This idea that God is somehow active and lifting us up in our moments of need and sorrow AND is also deeply present in our times of joy and in the relationships we have with one another was the dominant response that morning from the members of the congregation. Several people very freely spoke of difficult times in their lives during which, often through the caring of others, they simply knew and felt a caring, loving God. Several people gave very specific personal examples. Just listening to their testimonies was something I found most inspirational!

The agnostic or the atheist might suggest that these responses are not really good enough. He or she might render the opinion that the language the believer uses is really deeply conditioned by an upbringing or a catechesis built upon certain concepts of God. Indeed, if one has been subjected to years of church going, one has heard how much God cares for us. One has not only heard it but one has also quite frequently both spoken it and sung it.[1] And, one might say, if you have lived with this language long enough, it might become your built in reflexive response when you are con-fronted with mysteries the human mind cannot easily comprehend.

While one may thus find this conviction fairly difficult to PROVE, it was clear to me in sharing in this conversation is that these statements of faith were less about provability and more about heartfelt belief at the deepest personal level, a belief that transcends the language used to describe it. While that may be unsettling to anyone who approaches religious questions purely wedded to rational analysis, it does reflect the basic reality that, at core, any faith does require a leap of sorts, a recognition that one is in fact engaging in an act of faith.[2]

---

1   I think of the popular evangelical hymn 'God Will Take Care of You'

2   This concept of the 'leap of faith' is attributed to Soren Kierkegaard.

What I stated in affirming this as part of the conversation is that while faith contains this unique quality, faith need not be seen as something that runs contrary to reason. In other words, one CAN believe, as many in my congregation stated that day, in a God who KNOWS you and LOVES you deeply, while still recognizing that while the human mind might legitimately posit a reality that DOES this, the very language one uses to describe that divine reality falls short of both describing it and explaining all the details involved.

On the morning in which my church and I probed the mystery of God together, I was struck both by the depth and assurance of personal faith expressed within that congregation and the necessary sense that when we are speaking of God, we are in the realm of a mystery that is so difficult to either fully understand or adequately describe.

DISCUSSION QUESTIONS

1. What was your impression of this sermon? If you could say one thing about it, what would that be?
2. What, in your mind, is the relationship between faith and reason?
3. The author speaks of the importance of understanding the 'I –Thou' relationship when discussing God. What do you think?
4. In the context of the author's message, how do you evaluate the closing prayer he uses from Thomas Merton?

CHAPTER FIVE

Our next sermon in the series was preached on a Sunday in which our congregation celebrated the baptism of a beautiful little girl, the daughter of our former Music Director and her husband. As most baptisms are, it was a joyful occasion made even more festive that morning because of the special affection my congregation holds for this particular mom and her family. On the occasion of the celebration of this sacrament into the initiation of the life of the church, I decided that this was a good time to explore the very meaning of the act of baptism itself.

Now, to be honest, in mainline churches, most baptisms occur very early on in a child's life. It is also fair to say that a good number of baptisms also take place wherein the parents and other family members present are in a situation different from the family who celebrated this morning. Many baptismal celebrations are attended largely by family members and friends who rarely attend services of worship and the high probability is that the baptized child won't be attending worship all that often throughout her/his formative years as a child or a teen.

Whenever I officiate at a service of baptism, I try, in some way, to get the congregation to give some thought to both what is and what is NOT happening here. Recognizing that for many, bringing a child to baptism draws its significance from the reality that it is more tied to family tradition and heritage than to theological principle, I try to suggest ways that those present can examine what this baptism might potentially mean in both the life of the child as well as the life of everyone gathered for a few minutes that day in the sanctuary of a church.

Considering that this baptism occurred in the midst of this sermon series, I decided that it would be a good time to examine in more detail both the nature of baptism as well as some of the questions I have been asked concerning it.

This sermon in particular zoned in on questions I have been asked regarding the RELEVANCE of baptism. There is a certain element of *'so what?'* to be found within these questions: What difference does it make if you baptize a child but he/she opts not to make Christianity part of her/his life? Is there a way of preventing that? In this message, I try to offer a positive reminder that there are certain specific things that parents can do that, in essence, help them live out THEIR BAPTISMAL COMMITMENT to the child.

At most baptism ceremonies in most Christian churches these days, parents, family and friends are asked to make promises. In these promises, they vow to in effect create a climate within which a child can grow in Christian faith. Through this sermon, I attempt to give concrete suggestions for what creating that climate might look like, accepting all the while that even in doing all of this, there are no guarantees that an active church life will follow. Yet, even in saying that, I am most assured that it really is worth it.

WEEK FIVE SERMON

EPHESIANS 4:1-5, JOHN 6:24-35

'Pastor Bob, I have known so many children who were baptized and raised as Christians ... and then they grew up and they never go to church and Christianity is no longer a big part of their lives ... ... How can I prevent that? How can I raise my children to grow up to be Christians?'

Wow! Now is that not an appropriate question on a day in which we gather to celebrate the baptism of this beautiful girl? AND ... is it not a truly relevant question, one that cuts to the chase and gets to the very heart of what we have done and are doing here this morning?

For today Sarah and Bill made promises, the same promises they made when they came to this place with Nathan years ago — and the question for them and for any of us who have made these same promises is what will be the effect of that which they do today?

What difference will what they do and what we do with them make on the adult life of this wonderful little baby? What will be the relationship of this baptism, this immersion into the Christian community, on the life of this child as she grows?

Well, there is no easy way to answer this question, for sure, but this I will contend — that IF they take their responsibilities seriously, there WILL an effect and it WILL be long lasting … However, a caveat rests with it — it may not necessarily take the shape that was originally intended …

You see, when my parents brought me to baptism in January of 1953, they did so with the expectation that in raising me, in bringing me to church and exposing me to the faith in which I was baptized, I would grow up to be a churchgoer who would be both committed and quite likely would pass that faith along to others as well …

Now, I don't think they expected that my own particular journey of faith would take the twists and turns that it has or that I would reach some of the conclusions I have reached … conclusions that called into question some of which my own parents believed …

Even in a far more air tight society than ours, there were factors in my life that my parents or my religious education teachers could not control — influences upon my thinking, the natural evolution of my mind — … *and such will always be the case among those who seek to bring children up …*

AND — and this is essential — *ultimately for faith to really be faith — It must be something one embraces on one's own … …* Though we make promises to Julianne, though we give her this exposure to this faith and in essence give her the gift of faith — WE CANNOT GIVE HER FAITH, this is something into which she must grow … Nor can we guarantee that even if she were to come into a personal faith, it would take upon itself the same outward signs as ours ...

For there ARE some whose faith is deep who do not have a strong attachment to going to church or who were raised in strong Protestant homes who become Catholic ... or the other way around ... or so I am told ... BUT there are things we not only CAN do but I would suggest that we MUST do if we are to take seriously the promises that we as parents (and we as a church) make when we come to bring a child for baptism ...

But let's start by looking at parents ... First of all — Involve the child in the routine of church (and going to church with parents). Secondly, talk with the child about Jesus — Help the child get excited about not only who Jesus was, but what he taught ... of course, the Christmas and Easter stories are wonderful and easy to talk about, but go deeper and talk about what Jesus taught ... the parables, the Sermon on the Mount ... talk about what got Him crucified!!

Thirdly, help child get involved in Sunday School and then attending church after she attends Sunday School (or during). # 4 — encourage participation in youth activities, including service activities ... (It's delicate time — oftentimes, kids don't want to go, but it is worth pushing them in that direction!!) — ADVOCATE for good youth programs in your church ... AND ... When your child goes off to college (do you believe I am saying that this morning), encourage attendance at religious discussions and campus ministry activity —

I want to hear what you have to say ... for what I am saying is that YOU as parents and WE as a Christian community CAN HAVE a major impact and that we have a major responsibility to try our very best to have that impact upon the lives of these precious children whom we bring before the community ... ... whom we bring before one another, as Bill and Sarah have done today, as many of our own parents did in ages past, to receive this precious gift of baptism ... ...

For, on the day of our baptisms, we put on Jesus Christ — and on this day, we give that gift of Jesus to this beautiful and precious child ...

AMEN

LET'S TALK ...

THE CONVERSATION

There was a fairly immediate reaction when I opened the conversation up to the congregation that morning. This reaction centered on two responses this message evoked. Some participants freely acknowledged their sense of both bewilderment and resignation that even if you send children to Sunday School for years, there is no guarantee they will be church going adults. As a matter of fact, people were fairly free about giving personal examples, myself included!

On the other hand, there was a sense in the room that the specific examples I gave, while not providing any kind of insurance policy, had a value. As a matter of fact, some people who were in church that morning told me afterward that I had given them something to think about. I was most pleased that the conversation found its way toward emphasizing the serious connection between what was going on in church that morning and what would really happen in the faith life of that beautiful baby girl.

The reaction indicated to me that a strong need exists in the church for lofty ideals to be made concrete. Many times when I have asked the official questions during a baptism or confirmation ritual, I have thought to myself and often spoken aloud ... *'BUT WHAT DOES THIS REALLY MEAN?'* What are some practical ways that parents can put these noble ideals into practice? How can godparents be more than honorary bystanders in the child's life of faith? It is so important, and this came through in reactions both during the service and later on, that this important moment in the life of a family be far more than a lifeless tradition.

The seriousness with which the congregation engaged in these questions that morning was most uplifting. I noted to those present that churches need to do more reflection upon the applicability of the words we use to express such notable ideals. I encourage you, the reader, to consider the same.

DISCUSSION QUESTIONS

1. Some oppose infant baptism because **they believe baptism will have more meaning if it is freely chosen.** What do you think?
2. What is your opinion of the concrete suggestions the preacher used in this message?
3. In preparing couples and sponsors for baptism, should more emphasis be placed on the **WORDS** used in the promises they make? Explain.
4. How does your reaction compare with those in the congregation as described by the author?

CHAPTER SIX

When I went into the pulpit to deliver this sermon, it was the first time since I announced my resignation as pastor a few weeks prior, that I had this imminent sense that I would be leaving this beloved congregation soon. In my original written sermon text, I didn't even mention what came to me spontaneously as I was preaching. At one point in the sermon, I just looked up and said *'If there is one thing I have been trying to emphasize in all of my preaching here all of these years it is that IT ALL COMES DOWN TO JESUS!'* What I said in that moment was the heart of this sermon- and it wasn't even in the script!

As this message evolved, what began as a detailed analysis of the commonality of the universal religious quest ended up being my own personal testimony and witness to the centrality of Jesus in my life. The sermon itself was an attempt to place individual religious practice and response within the broader context of why human beings respond religiously. Throughout my career as both a religious educator and a pastor, I have found most helpful a simple definition about religion I learned a long time ago. In this brief description, all religion is seen as a basic response to the mystery of life, in particular those unknown areas surrounding human origin, ultimate destiny and everyday meaning.

As a Christian pastor in a pluralistic culture, I find it essential that I help people see the profound connection between what we do as Christians and what other people who happen not to be Christian seek to do as well. In doing so, I am hopeful that people will understand that there is human commonality in our mutual quest for what is right and true and meaningful i.e, at core, there are amazing similarities between why Christians do what we do and why those of other perspectives do as well.

The flip side of this is that an openness to pluralism can often be seen as an unwillingness to declare what one claims as the priority of one's own perspective in one's life. I believe that this tension is exhibited in this sermon as I seek to make clear the importance of Jesus and what He taught to how I frame my own responses to questions so clearly complex and shrouded in the unknown.

In my view, in doing so, the preacher moves from academic teacher about religion into her/his role as proclaimer of God's message for the current time and place and for the real lives of those who happen to be sitting in the pews. As I constructed this sermon, it was clear to me that I wanted to do whatever I could to encourage people to really take a fresh look at Jesus. My personal realization that I was coming to the end of my time in this church as pastor to this congregation led me to a greater sense of urgency. When it comes to 'those things that really matter,'[1] such urgency is not necessarily a bad thing!

WEEK SIX SERMON

LUKE 6:17-25; 27-36;41-42;46-49

'Pastor Bob, in your opinion, what is religion really all about? What is most important to know and to pass along to others?'

Now, that, my friends, is an incredibly relevant question, wouldn't you say? It is relevant because this question of BELIEV-ING- of identifying those values that are most important in our lives- is one which all of us must face ...

It is a meaningful question also because in this world of ours, there is a wide variety of ANSWERS to the question of believing, isn't there?

---

1   See Romans 2:18. Even in translations that do not use these exact words, the meaning is implied!

You know, the very best definition of RELIGION that I ever heard is a very simple one — -RELIGION IS OUR PERSONAL RESPONSE TO THE MYSTERY OF LIFE.

It's a good definition for two reasons — 1. It gets at the PERSONAL (it is unique to each of us and comes out of our experience) and 2. It acknowledges that life is a mystery containing within itself even more mystery — mysteries of ORIGIN, DESTINY … and ultimately, the mystery of MEANING —

And, as we well know, from our look at the religious world around us, there is a wide variety of RESPONSES to all of these mysteries — hence, the variety of religions and religious approaches — Islam, Judaism, Christianity, Buddhism, Hinduism (the oldest of them all), agnosticism, atheism and all kinds of unique other approaches, often connected, if somewhat loosely, to some of the more widely known traditions …

So, then , to ask the questions — what is religion really all about? What is important to know and pass on to others? – to ask these questions AND TO ANSWER THEM … is to really engage in the process of narrowing down all of these big questions, isn't it? — narrowing them down while ,at the same time, paying profound respect to their enormity — and paying due humility to the limitations of our human minds …

BUT … LET ME TRY …

This morning, I have freely chosen to be in the sanctuary of a church, haven't I? A church, by definition, is a gathering of Christians — the term church is a Christian (New Testament term) — Last week, I heard on the news something about a service at an 'Islam church' … I have heard people say they are going to 'Jewish churches' — These are inaccurate uses of the word CHURCH …

Not only am I here voluntarily as part of a Christian church but I also have willingly accepted the responsibility of being your pastor and thus of conducting services such as today's baptisms, correct? So, what I am telling you, through these actions, is that, of all the many answers out there and all of these different religious approaches, what it comes down to for me is pretty basic — IT ALL COMES DOWN TO JESUS!

Please understand ... in saying this, I do not either state or imply any disrespect for other religions ... In fact, I would argue that Christian teaching is totally compatible with and in some cases inspired by other religions ... (Jesus' teaching just could not be without the Jewish faith which He practiced!) What I AM saying is that, in my view, the heart of soul of the answer to these questions — What's religion all about? What do we want to pass on? — can be found by looking at WHAT JESUS TAUGHT ...

I am pleased to declare without hesitation that for me — Jesus is MY WAY, He is MY TRUTH and, He is, most certainly, my VERY LIFE — 'To live is Christ,' Paul declared in his words to the Phillip-ians, words to which I can only say 'AMEN'!

And so, the initial questions move deeper then — What is Jesus all about? What about HIM do we want to pass on? And this is where things can get complicated for so often Jesus is hidden under layers of both church and public traditions and rules and laws and customs that have accrued down through the centuries ... making it extremely hard for us to do what we must do and just get to Jesus!

You see Jesus is not a Congregationalist or a Baptist or a Catholic ... He's not the personal spokesman for the Roman Empire or the folks governing Puritan New England! NO ... Jesus is JESUS ...

AND get to Jesus we must ... for the sake of this movement we call Christianity ... and for the sake of those whom we baptize in His name! So, in answering this question, I will say that a place to start is found right here in these words from the Gospel of Luke (found in other places in the Bible too), words which capture the heart and the essence of what Jesus taught ...

Read these words from Jesus found in Luke and then go back and read Matthew 5-7 (Sermon on the Mount) and then read this and here is what you will find:

1. An incredible sense of our CLOSENESS to God- who created and loves us —
2. The powerful connection between what God does for YOU — and what you MUST do for others — God loves, forgives, looks past your faults, treats you with mercy — so must you!
3. A profound regard for those in NEED — 'Blest are the poor, the neglected, the weeping' — a commitment to reversing the plight of those on life's margins …
4. This sense, that when all is said and done … No matter how bad life gets, God will take care of you — YOU AND I ARE GOD'S ULTIMATE CONCERN … We who weep will one day laugh. We who mourn shall someday rejoice —

My friends, the message of Jesus, the ethic of Jesus, poses stumbling blocks for those who argue in favor of taking care of # 1 and disregarding the poor or whose range of concern is limited to their families or those 'of their kind' or who feel that the answer to violence … is simply VIOLENCE … and who see vengeance as a motivation for policy and action … You see, if you really get near Jesus and take Jesus seriously, you come to understand why down through the years He has been covered up by kingdoms and nations … and even churches — and why He has been hidden by power, be it ideological or theological …

BUT … since you asked the question, I have given an answer — If you are talking about the HEART and the SOUL and the CORE of religion, a philosophical mindset and a lifestyle worth passing on to these precious children and worth living yourself …

If you are looking for all of that, I vote that you turn to Jesus!

AMEN
Let's talk …

THE CONVERSATION

On the morning I preached this sermon, there were a couple of guests in the congregation who responded quite positively to the opportunity to make comments and ask questions after they heard a preacher's message! My sense is that when one sits in church and listens to a preacher, so much is happening inside. One word, phrase or idea can trigger something that can lead one to in depth consideration of matters one has either not really reflected upon or has done so in not much more than a cursory manner.

As I opened up the conversation to the gathered congregation, two friends who happened to be visiting our church that morning raised questions that they had been thinking about for quite a while. They both wanted to pursue what I said about the universal questions to which religion responds and where the current impasse and conflict between Christians and Muslims fits into the picture. In raising these questions, these two women helped open up for us the opportunity to look at the reality of interfaith relations in what has already become a divided, war torn twenty first century.

In my estimation, the horrific terrorist attacks and the exacerbation of ill will resulting from our nation's involvement in wars in Afghanistan and Iraq, have also led to great difficulty in establishing and maintaining a climate of interfaith respect among Christians and Muslims. Sadly, this ill will, in my view, has been made even worse by the terrible behavior of extremist Christians who have painted the picture of extreme Islamic terrorism as the real face of this long standing, historic faith.

I tried to take the opportunity, in response to their questions and inquiries, to establish the importance of renewed understanding of Islam and to reiterate what President George W. Bush said in response to the horrors of 9/11. In a famous statement just days after these terrible attacks, President Bush distinguished the despicable actions of those who committed these crimes against humanity from the heart and soul of Islamic faith, declaring at one point in his message that 'Islam means peace.'[1]

I also suggested that what we, as local Christian congregations, really need to do is continue to offer opportunities to learn about and meet with those whose perspectives are different from our own. I referred to historic misunderstandings between Protestants and Catholics and Christians and Jews. The congregation seemed receptive to my response and I was extremely grateful to these women for raising a practical question that cuts to the chase and causes one to really explore the practical applicability of that which one might profess.

I was also quite pleased that as part of this conversation, other individuals noted their appreciation for my focus on the teachings of Jesus. This is a message I also received later that week from those post sermon 'conversations' that occur via email.[2] As I explained that morning, one of my regular messages over these years is that Jesus does not always get a very good press from those of us who claim to be His followers. Quite often, our perception of Christianity and thus of Jesus is filtered through what preachers and teachings and church doctrine have taught us about Him. My concern that that '*the essential Jesus*' and His core teachings all too often get lost in what quite frequently becomes an extremely tangled web.

Of all of our post sermon conversations, this was most certainly one of the most profound! As a congregation, we are indebted to the contributions of those who were present in that sanctuary that morning, including our guests. In making the preached Word accessible to conversation, one also makes possible the hearing of different voices, voices who may just happen to grace our pews on

---

1   In my view, this statement needs to be held up as a positive example and as a necessary antidote to much of the hate talk surrounding Christian-Muslim relations.

2   This is one of the exciting possibilities that emanates from this kind of a series, a possibility I urge preachers to explore! Other means include the use of social media technologies such as FACEBOOK and TWITTER, as well as the use of blogs to which people can respond.

any given Sunday morning, voices that can challenge and move us to deeper levels in our growth.

DISCUSSION QUESTIONS

1. Do you think one can be both tolerant of religious pluralism and a strong advocate of Christianity?
2. What is your view of the current state of interfaith relations?
3. Some people think that appreciating other religions leads one to become indifferent about the unique claim of Christianity. What do you think?
4. What is your opinion of how the author identifies the core teachings of Jesus?
5. Do you agree that Jesus' teachings have been filtered by preachers, teachers and doctrine in ways that draw one away from what Jesus really taught or do you think the author is being too simplistic in his assertion? Give examples and explain!

Chapter Seven

This seventh sermon in our summer series was delivered in a beautiful outdoor location in the heart of the wonderful little Connecticut town in which I had served for a bit over a decade. It was our annual outdoor service on the occasion of the town's annual Old Home Day weekend. Old Home Day is, in my view, a magnificent local tradition established long ago by one of the church's former pastors. The essence of this local tradition is that on the third Saturday in August, those who have had any connection with Union, Connecticut gather together and renew these ties.

Since our church, the only congregation of any kind in this town of slightly over eight hundred, is so intricately connected with the community, it is fitting that we do a special service which affirms the importance of this community in our common lives, including our lives as members of this church. It is interesting that as this weekend drew near and with it my recognition that this would be my last Old Home Day service enveloped me as well, that I was drawn back to questions I had been asked many times over the years not only by people in Union, but also by those with whom I have worked and others whom I have known in the different arenas in which I have lived my life.

In answering this question- '*What is it like to be a minister?*' and even more concretely '*What's it like to be a pastor?*,' I was naturally taken back to all of the concrete realities I had lived and all the relationships that accompanied them through the years I had served in this great community. I was also aware of some phenomenal writing about this topic I have had the opportunity to read over the years, in particular Eugene Petersen's engaging work simply entitled *The Pastor.*[1]

What struck me most through my thinking and my reminiscing was yet another concrete conviction I have been emphasizing

---

1 See Eugene Petersen, *The Pastor* (New York: Harper One, 2011).

through all of my years in this particular pulpit, one which I emphasized in my candidating sermon in my new congregation just a few weeks prior. As I prepared this sermon, I tried to move it in the direction of a renewed call for members of a local congregation to really embrace the concept of the 'priesthood of all believers' and to see the local church as not so much about the pastor, but rather about pastor and other members of the congregation REALLY working together!

I found it most revealing that as I came to the end of my time at one church and began my ministry at another, my point of emphasis so happened to be the very same!

Week Seven Sermon

1 Peter 2:4-9, John 1: 43-47

'Pastor Bob, what's it like to be a minister?'

That, my friends, is a question I am asked quite frequently-by people of different ages, in different contexts and each of them with their own unique perceptions of how I might answer ...

'Pastor Bob, what's it like to be a minister and to serve as a pastor?'

The simple, honest and most direct answer is this: **It's great ... There, sermon over! Well, not quite so easily!!**

Seriously, this question has come front and center for me in these last few weeks as I have been preparing to leave my ministry after 11 ½ years as your pastor here in Union and prepare for the next chapter in my church life ... I've been thinking about it a lot!

And as the question has burst into the forefront of both my feelings and my thoughts, so too have the memories come flooding back that offer the most real and honest answer to the question.

Memories of busy, hectic Sunday mornings, of special events, dinners, Holly Day Fairs, Balloon Sundays, Christmas Eves, reminders of intense meetings with tough decisions to make and with so much to do ... Reminiscences about days such as this — Old Home Days shared-when those of us present have a special feeling, a sense of shared identity, a knowledge that there is a bond between us and among us, a bond we most assuredly did not create on our own ...

What's it like to be a minister? To serve as a pastor?

Well, underlying all the hours of preparing sermons, of picking out music (lots of music), of planning youth retreats, sending out emails, talking at length and the like — underlying all of this is the privilege that comes from the relationships you share with people as their minister — and the enormous, yet precious burden, you bear because people turn to you expecting something good and helpful from you, in their moments of greatest joy-and in their times of darkest sorrow!

To baptize a baby (or someone older), to confirm one of our youth, to wish you well and shake your hand or embrace you on a Sunday morning when the service is over, to stand before a couple and declare them married — to see the love and the hope in their eyes ... that is all joy ! And to sit by a bedside and join your hands to the hands of a family as they fear the very worst, to stand by a grave or in a church or a funeral home, to try to utter words that express what THIS LIFE has meant to these people before you ... those are the times of the most profound and the deepest sorrow ...

YET, even in the sorrow, there is the HOPE, the hope that is based on a promise we have been told, a hope founded upon a faith both incredible and reasonable at one and the same time- FAITH — THE SUBSTANCE OF THAT WHICH WE HOPE FOR AND THE EVIDENCE OF THINGS NOT SEEN, the Bible says- a promise that there is a God who created us — out of love and with a purpose, that this God not only will not abandon us in our sorrow, but will bring us into a realm of joy that, left on our own, we could not even begin to imagine!

So, there's my answer to what it's like to be a minister, to serve as a pastor- what I've just said really says it all for me ...

BUT THE SERMON'S STILL NOT OVER!

You know, as I prepare to leave here and ready myself to move on to a new and different place in our relationship with each other, I find myself trying to emphasize certain things — you know how it is when you have limited time and want to cram it all in? Last week, in the middle of my sermon (wasn't even in my text!), I said that if there is one thing from my years as your pastor I want to leave you as a message it's that when all is said and done, IT ALL COMES DOWN TO JESUS — and I implored the congregation that morning to take this seriously and to PAY ATTENTION not just to all these teachings ABOUT Jesus that often HIDE JESUS ... but to pay attention to JESUS HIMSELF!!

This morning, I have but another POINT OF EMPHASIS — something I have said hundreds of times since I became your pastor here ... AND I am about to say it again! *'Pastor Bob, what is it like to be a minister?'* — Well, I have answered the question, but I am here to tell you something else ... I'm not the only minister up here in this beautiful place this morning —

We, who seek to take seriously who Jesus is and what Jesus taught — WE ARE ALL MINISTERS — that is what this reading from Peter is all about — it's everything we believe about 'the priesthood of all believers' ... Without denying the unique and special responsibilities that I and your future pastors shall have and without downplaying the importance of a pastor working hard to fulfill those responsibilities ... I am here to tell you that here in this church, right here in this little town, inside the walls of your home, among those whom you love and who come to visit you, across the street in this school, in your office or your classroom, among your friends or with those who might pull your chain and drive you a little nuts ... WHEREVER YOU ARE ... NO MATTER WHAT

YOUR AGE MAY BE ... YOU CARRY JESUS WITH YOU ... YOU ARE A MINISTER OF THE GOSPEL ...

Just as long ago, something wonderful came out of Nazareth, so too shall it come out of Union!-FOR YOU, WHO CELE- BRATE THIS WEEKEND IN THIS GREAT LITTLE TOWN — YOU ARE A MINISTER OF THE GOSPEL. AND FOR SOME PEOPLE, DEAR FRIENDS ... YOU ARE THE ONLY GOSPEL THAT THEY SHALL EVER READ!

AND ... So, dear friends, I will end by asking you this — What's it like to be a minister? What is it like to carry Jesus Christ? AMEN

THE CONVERSATION

Leaving a church one loves is not an easy thing. And, while I knew that people were very supportive of my decision and were most appreciative of the years I spent in ministry with them, I also was aware of the fact that there is such a reality as honest human emotion at work in the relationship between pastor and congre- gation. It is not overly dramatic to say that as I looked out at the congregation that morning, I saw young people who were infants when I first arrived, so many people with whom I have met and consulted, survivors of those loved ones at whose funerals I offici- ated, women and men who connected with and became members of this church during these years in which I was their pastor.

While my sermon was an attempt to look at the reality of the total church in light of the historic conviction about our shared priesthood, I suppose it was inevitable that something might come out about the fact that I was leaving — and it did. As a matter of fact, someone expressed gratitude to me during this public conver- sation after the sermon while, at the very same time, holding back tears. To be honest, it was a bit of an uncomfortable position to be in and while I wondered momentarily *'Whose idea was it to do a dialogue sermon?'* (knowing fully well it was mine!), I also quickly realized that this is the stuff of real Christian community and that it is quite OK for people to express their feelings about the nature of relationships within that community.

I sensed in the immediate moment that morning that some people needed to say something positive about my ministry and that it would be acceptable for me to just allow them to say it. I think there were some feelings simmering under the surface that simply needed to come out. Fortunately, only two or three people opted to do so which thus provided me the opportunity to move this message back to where I wanted. It was not long before I was able to reiterate that if we as a congregation have been pleased with our development over these last few years, we need to reflect back and realize that this church is what it is because we have assumed a SHARED RESPONSIBILITY for it ... TOGETHER ...

DISCUSSION QUESTIONS

1. What do you think of the author's selection of question for this sermon?
2. What is your reaction to the discomfort he felt as the dialogue opened up and turned to his work as a minister?
3. In looking at the sermon, what might you have said in response to how he presented the concept of 'priesthood of all believers'?
4. In your view, how important is a pastor in a local congregation? Please explain in detail.

CHAPTER EIGHT

In deciding how I would conclude this summer long series of messages and conversations, I rather easily determined that the best place to end is with an exploration of the afterlife. There were several reasons underpinning this decision. First and foremost among them was the reality that as a pastor who has had to conduct many funerals and work closely with those who are grieving, I have been expected to say something about the afterlife on many occasions, situations in which people are seeking some words of comfort and assurance. In addition, in many private conversations with individuals both preparing for their deaths or dealing with the loss of their beloved, I have been asked about life after death. A pastor is expected, I suppose, to be able to provide some kind of answer to what one could arguably contend is life's greatest mystery of all.

In wrapping up this particular series, preached at a time of my own personal transition and that of my congregation, I felt it important to address one of the major inquiries I, along with most pastors, receive, in a manner that is faithful to the humanity any pastor shares with her/his congregation as well as to my pastoral responsibility to bear witness to that which I honestly believe.

The occasion of being overwhelmed with the task of moving a slew of books from one office to another over the last few weeks of this summer provided me the opportunity to confront an underlying reality in the pastor-congregant relationship. While the pastor is rightfully expected to have strong knowledge of the Bible, church teaching and its history, the pastor at the very same time is a human being whose breadth and depth of reading and reflection provides no assurance that he or she has the right answers to the greatest mysteries that confront us as mere mortals.

On the other hand, I think it is fair to say that people turn to their pastors to provide them some insights into realities that are intensely profound and complicated. Thus, in the context of this message, I found that it was extremely important that, without asserting any degree of special knowledge, I nonetheless should 'bear witness' to that which I believe, not because I fully grasp what this notion of eternal life is all about, but rather because we all need people of faith to point us in directions that might help us make sense out of that which we naturally perceive as completely beyond our grasp.

Affirming one's faith and expressing one's willingness to take a reasoned, plausible leap is an important task in both the life and the preaching of anyone charged with pastoral responsibility. In bearing witness, in this case to a vision of what life after death might be, the preacher, in essence, addresses the questions with which he/she is confronted. The preacher allows the hearer to 'listen in' on the very process she/he undergoes at her/his very core and to catch a glimpse of how the preacher has arrived at the conviction she/he proclaims- in my case, on this particular day in this one sanctuary in a little quiet corner of God's big wide world.

WEEK EIGHT SERMON

REVELATION 21:1-8, REVELATION 22:1-5, JOHN 14:13

'Pastor Bob, what do you believe about the afterlife? What can you tell us about life after death?'

Now, how is that for an easy topic on the final week of a sermon series? Let me begin to even try to give an answer by telling you this-

If you were to walk downstairs to my office this morning and look up at the bookshelves, they would seem awfully empty-especially if you have ever spent time in my office and were familiar with the overflow of books that rendered those shelves a wee untidy, shall we say! You see, last weekend, with the help of my son Stephen and my wife, I began the process of taking the belongings out of my office here, including hundreds of books, and moving them over to my new office in Manchester …

Now, you might be thinking — 'OK, so what's the point?' When anyone leaves a job, he or she has to clean out one's work-space … How is he going to make a sermon out of this? Well, let me tell you — a lot of books went into those boxes that my son carried- volumes containing the kinds of things that ministers study, that we study to help us serve our congregations — books about God, about the Bible and the history of the church, as well as other religions, books containing indepth teaching about some of the most difficult and perplexing questions that fill our human minds — extensive pieces of writing that probe the mysteries of life — and of death — and of the kind of life that might exist after we die …

Ministers read these books to help shape our sermons, develop our teaching, and offer suggestions and consolation to those whom we serve — But do you know what? I and others who are profes-sionals in the 'world of religion,' despite all of the reading we may have done, with due respect to all of the thinking and speculation that may go in to the work we do, and with deep regard for the faith that we possess, we are all on an equal playing field with those who have never turned one page in any of those volumes-

Oh, we might be able to tell you the different things the Bible teaches. We might be able to tell you what great thinkers have thought down through the ages and we might even be able to help correct some of the silliness that has developed around these topics — BUT WHEN PUSH COMES TO SHOVE — the exact answer to what happens after people die remains to a great extent, a mystery, something we don't completely know …

Each of us, my friends, is on a level playing field in this re-gard — we are human beings, not God- and we don't know all of the answers … We are human beings … and we WONDER … .we wonder about that which we don't completely know … Now, having said this, does that mean that we can say nothing? That I, as a pastor, have nothing to offer you that can make sense of these mysteries, that my only honest answer to these questions found at the top of this sermon can be nothing other than a simple 'I DON'T KNOW!'?

Now, listen carefully, OK?

Did you hear that first question? What do you **BELIEVE** about the afterlife? I think that anyone asking this question-and many have asked it through these years- believes that this is a pretty important question, one about which a pastor may have given some serious thought — and I HAVE — my friends, I REALLY HAVE …

I BELIEVE that the God who made me wants me to live forever — and when I say me, I mean YOU as well. I believe that when you look into all of these books and when you cut to the chase and get to the heart of the Bible and when you see Jesus, once dead, declared ALIVE — THAT is what God has in mind for all of us when our journey has ended — a LIFE beyond this LIFE, a life containing a joy and a happiness beyond description, a life that builds upon everything good in this one — the LOVE, the RELATIONSHIPS we have with one another, a life that takes all that is good and magnifies it in a way we cannot even begin now to understand —

'What can you tell me about life after death, Pastor Bob?'

Well, I can tell you that I believe with all of my heart that Jesus is already there and that His words are really true — that He goes to prepare us a place, so that where He is, so too shall we someday be! And I can tell you that many others are with Him as well in that place that He has prepared, a PLACE that takes us well beyond what we might mean when we say place, that is unlike any other place to which we have ever been, while, at the same time, very much like it as well —

I will tell also you as well that you and I have known a lot of those folk who are ALSO in that place, who have taken up the invitation to follow ... *AND there are more than likely people there you would not expect ... AND who might not even have expected it of themselves as well ...*

My friends, much of what I believe and offer those I serve is built upon what I don't know as well — I believe there is such a reality as HELL — I have no idea whether anyone's there — for I trust in a redeeming God, though I am well aware, from what I know of history, including that which we are now making each day, that there are those who might never seek redemption and whose evil can only be explained by the presence of an EVIL which, in the end, refuses to accept the loving grace of God ... .

So, then, as my books have been transported to a different place, to be opened again in situations I cannot even begin to predict right now, I realize that while they don't offer every certain answer, they have guided me on what is ultimately a journey of faith — and in their reading, illumined by the experience that has been my life- with its ups and its downs and its joy and its sorrows — it is THIS FAITH that I am so glad to pass on to you as your pastor-

Jesus Christ is Risen! He has gone to prepare a place for you and for those whom you love — as well as for those whom you really might not think about loving at all!-

At the end of this series of summer sermons, is there any better place to end? Jesus Christ is Risen! We who call ourselves the church- we are an Easter people! We are an Easter people ... and ALLELUIA, ... Alleluia is truly our song!

AMEN

THE CONVERSATION

If I had not brought it to closure, this conversation could have gone on for a very long time. It wasn't long after I had finished and asked if the congregation had anything to ask or say, that hands went up in virtually every pew. The conversation went off in all kinds of different directions. Some asserted that my statements of faith reflected their own. Others wondered about the practice of cremation. Still others inquired about those who did not believe in Jesus and where they were in the big eternal picture.

The variety of responses and the way we explored the multiplicity of positions existent even among those who believe in life after death both reaffirmed for me that this side of Paradise, we really do see very, very dimly, yet also that there is an inherent value in one's fidelity to the belief that beyond this realm of the known in which we live, into what we describe as the realm of the unknown … in both realms, God is there!

This after sermon time was a good way to end this summer series. We who gathered in that little church that morning were talking about something that was all going to happen to all of us someday. For no one there, be he or she in pew or pulpit, was going to escape the inevitability of death. Likewise, I am not sure anyone there that morning has been immune from the intrusion of death in our ordinary lives throughout the course of that time in which we have already lived.

As this conversation ended and we joined in the singing of a hymn, I was struck by the reality that in this very act of questioning and sharing, in the stories we told and even the doubts that we expressed, we as a Christian community, a local church, were truly bearing witness not only to whatever happens beyond these earthly existences of ours, but also to the very presence of that 'beyond in our midst' of which Bonhoeffer writes, that within us which inspires us to examine these matters at all. It was a wonderful way to finish what I truly believe was a wonderful summer, a final summer for me in this, a wonderful place!

DISCUSSION QUESTIONS

1. Our author contends that there is a value is sharing the fact that one really doesn't know the whole picture. In your view,

is that a good thing for a preacher to share? Is it harmful to witnessing to faith?

2. Does the contemporary church suffer from not spending enough time and energy thinking about the afterlife?
3. Is there something in the process of moving out of the office that serves as metaphor for what the author says in this sermon?
4. Is it helpful or harmful to open up questions of this complexity in a time of Sunday worship?
5. If you had to make a statement or ask a question about today's sermon, what would it be?

CONCLUSION:
SO MUCH OLDER THEN

In these previous eight chapters, you, the reader, have been exposed to eight different short sermons. These sermons were intended to, in some way, contribute to each present hearer's interaction with a living God. These messages had as their purpose a 'breaking open' of the Word, so that what appears on the written page from a time so long ago has relevance in the lives of the hearer in this present moment, becoming in effect a 'present revelation,'[1] a truly spiritual moment, right here and right now.

What must never be lost in this process is that, while in the structure of this sermon series, the activity of the Spirit, as it were, in the life of the hearer, benefitted whomever was present, *he or she who assumes the role of preacher is in fact a hearer as well.* The preacher is able to preach well only if she or he has interacted both with the biblical text and, most importantly, with that text in deep relationship with her/his own life.

It is trite and simplistic to say that the preacher at worship assumes a different role from that of the academic theological scholar. Yet, while trite indeed, it is also quite true. As one crafts a sermon, one allows the text to interact with the totality of one's life-its questions, its presumed answers, its disappointments, its hopes, even its doubts! While this may seem to be an aside, it is important for me to say that this is why I truly abhor the idea of simply pulling a sermon I have already preached out of the file and repeating it. I believe strongly that even if I preached about the Prodigal Son, for example, three years ago from this particular date, I am not the same as I was then. Since the time of that earlier proclamation, I have had new life experiences. Where in the year 2009, I may have focused on the older brother, perhaps this year, I am feeling more

---

1   See Gabriel Moran. *The Present Revelation*(New York: McGraw- Hill, 1972).

like the younger son and maybe next time, I will be tuned in to the actions of the father. This would happen, of course, because of what I have gone through in MY OWN LIFE in that time leading up to MY OWN hearing of this Biblical text. The preacher can't be a good preacher without being a good hearer, hearing the Word of God in the HERE and NOW!

If I had preached sermons on these topics in 1989 when I was first ordained in the Catholic Church or in 1978 had I gone from college straight to seminary and then on to ordination, these sermons would have been so different. Without going into a lengthy autobiography here, suffice it to say that I grew up in a world surrounded by a lot of religious certainty, where the religious orthodoxy in which I was raised dominated my own religious formation. In my early years, even into adolescence, there was a lot of certainty in my life—about God, about Jesus, about how and why I was created, as well as for all of the available options for how I would spend my life after I die. There were well developed catechism answers and a library of concrete examples acquired over the years for use by those experienced in catechetical formation. As a beneficiary of the work of dedicated religious sisters, I was well schooled in these orthodoxies as well as the stories that buttressed them!

As a teenager in the tumultuous era known affectionately to some and disparagingly to others as 'the 60's,' I began to question many of my old assumptions and orthodoxies, yet found myself replacing them with a new set of absolutes, especially with regard to the relationship between religious belief and political action. I embraced a new orthodoxy based on the premise that, when all is said and done, there is really a right way and a wrong way to look at the Vietnam war, the military and the role of government in our lives. If truth be told, many of my generation found it hard to accept that those who did not think and vote the way we did, truly did not have as good a sense of what really constitutes right and wrong.

By the time I got to the pulpit in the summer of 2012 and as I responded homiletically to questions people had asked me, I was quite aware that their questions are the questions I had asked myself as well and that the answers that to some of those questions, which might have been absolute at many given times, were not exactly quite as clear. I knew that I had changed over the course of the years and that while my core beliefs remained intact, I had come to see variables and nuances in life that weren't so clear in years before.

As a near sixty year old when I went to that pulpit, I had experienced the death of my parents, the birth and growth of three of my children, thirty two years of marriage, and a lot of years behind closed doors counseling a lot of people in a good number of difficult situations, situations in which ethical decisions were not always easy and clear cut. I had learned on a visceral level what I had learned in my head years before-*that what appeared to be absolute in the abstract was often quite ambiguous in the concrete.* As I entered this sermon series, I was a man increasingly aware that, in a flash, I had gone through middle age and that, to so many with whom I shared each work day, including most of my bosses these days, I was really an elder! *Good grief, how did that ever happen?,* I thought!

I realized as well what many people my age do. I recognized that when I look at the obituary pages, there are a lot of people there around my age whose names are printed there and that the numerical gap is no longer that great between me and those just a bit older who happen be at that average age at which people die. While experienced enough as both pastor and human being to know that death can come at quite young an age as well, I also have enough of a rudimentary knowledge of statistics to know where I place on the charts and the graphs!

Even deeper, as a pastoral leader, I have grown to develop an acute awareness that, even as I am a 'go to' person for answers, there are so many answers I don't know. I really don't know what eternal life is EXACTLY like right now for my mother or father or the grandmothers I knew and loved or for all of those beloved individuals whose funerals I have conducted, though I believe most deeply in eternal life. I cannot answer with absolute certainty the specifics of God's will, what God really looks like and where God really stands on the political questions that have so often occupied my mind.

Now, there are some who might read this would might say '*We've got a problem here. We have a preacher to whom people turn who can't give them what they need and who cannot provide them the assurance for which they yearn.*' I look at this differently!

I believe that as the certainty about some of these absolutes has waned, as so many doctrines with which I have filled my head have been held up to examination, at the very same time, my faith has grown. It is less a faith in my absolute knowledge about the Absolute and more a faith that the Absolute, that which we name God, is far deeper and greater than we can ever imagine. It is less a faith in doctrinal purity about Jesus and Christology, though I consider theological articulation important, and it is more about my complete fascination with the One whom I consider to be my way, my truth and my life and, yes, the One I acknowledge as my Savior, even as I am most acutely aware that I'm in need of a lot of saving!

At the end of the day, I have rediscovered an amazing story from the Fourth Gospel, the Gospel according to John. [1] In this fascinating conversation with Peter, set as it were in a time that transcended time, Jesus concludes by telling a very complex Peter that '*When you were younger, you used to fasten your belt and do whatever you wish.*' (I get that. I really do and I would suspect a lot of that came out in my preaching!). And then Jesus adds something else to his mercurial friend: '*But when you grow old, you will stretch out your hands, and someone else will fasten a belt around you and take you where you do not wish to go.*'

It is easier than any alternative, we often think, to live in certainty, to build walls that protect our ways of thinking, fortresses that surround us, illusions that underpin our lives. [2] It is easier to shield ourselves from the questions, questions that could shatter the structures we have taken the time to build. But helping us confront these questions is what Jesus ia ll about. And, in doing this, He is

---

1   See John 21 with an emphasis on verse 18 in particular.
2   I think of the Paul Simon song 'I Am A Rock.'

telling us something incredibly profound about God — *'Stretch out your hands. TRUST. All that good stuff about children in the Bible ... Calling God 'Abba.' Just like a Dad or a Mom ... It's really all about TRUST ... '*

Might you and I be able to trust God enough, a God whom we cannot fully imagine or understand or describe ... can we trust God enough to take this leap of faith, really, and to affirm in our healthily childlike hearts that where we think we would rather not go–THAT is where we will be fulfilled- beyond the walls of our illusions, those ways in which we have been conditioned, beyond all of the confines that custom and tradition and culture imposes?

Dare I say that wherever that is, God just happens to be there ... and God will be forever ...

Dare I say, with Augustine of yore,[1] that where that is, we knew it all along, though we may have built walls to protect ourselves from really knowing ... ?

Dare I say, really, that I can't really speak for you but I believe that I can for me ... that my orthodoxy and reflexive sense of assurance has given way to something far deeper, to that which provides the foundation that underlies all these wonderful words of faith I've used so often in this increasingly lengthening while, at the same time, ever shortening, life.?

Dare I say that I both really get and fully embrace those words of the poet songwriter whose lyrics I have heard and sung so often, words that have inspired me to craft words of my own, words I have shared with others, as I've encouraged them in turn to share their own words with me, all with an eye to the Word which our language just never completely captures, a Word from beyond, from the beyond that really resides right here, right here in our very midst: **'Oh, but I was so much older then, I'm younger than that now'[2]**

---

1 This observation is inspired by Augustine's noted observation that 'Our hearts are restless until they rest in Thee.'

2 From Bob Dylan's *My Back Pages*. Please see the epigraph.

ALSO FROM ENERGION PUBLICATIONS

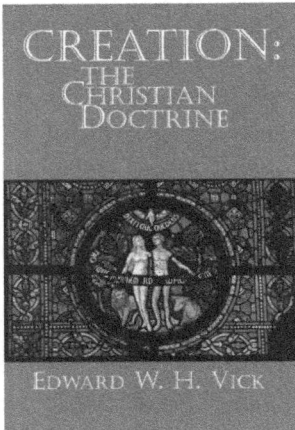

... an outstanding resource in Christian theology, one to which I expect to return many, many times.

Rev. Dr. Robert D. LaRochelle.

ALSO BY BOB LAROCHELLE

I highly recommend this book to those who are interested in learning from one man's courageous and joyful journey.

The Rev. Albert R. Cutié
Priest-in-Charge
Church of the Resurrection
Biscayne Park, FL

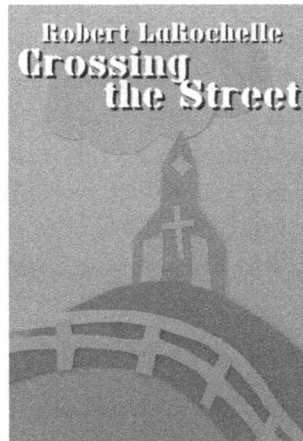

MORE FROM ENERGION PUBLICATIONS

Personal Study

Finding My Way in Christianity	Herold Weiss	$16.99
Holy Smoke! Unholy Fire	Bob McKibben	$14.99
The Jesus Paradigm	David Alan Black	$17.99
When People Speak for God	Henry Neufeld	$17.99
The Sacred Journey	Chris Surber	$11.99

Christian Living

Faith in the Public Square	Robert D. Cornwall	$16.99
Grief: Finding the Candle of Light	Jody Neufeld	$8.99
Crossing the Street	Robert LaRochelle	$16.99

Bible Study

Learning and Living Scripture	Lentz/Neufeld	$12.99
From Inspiration to Understanding	Edward W. H. Vick	$24.99
Luke: A Participatory Study Guide	Geoffrey Lentz	$8.99
Philippians: A Participatory Study Guide	Bruce Epperly	$9.99
Ephesians: A Participatory Study Guide	Robert D. Cornwall	$9.99

Theology

Creation in Scripture	Herold Weiss	$12.99
Creation: the Christian Doctrine	Edward W. H. Vick	$12.99
The Politics of Witness	Allan R. Bevere	$9.99
Ultimate Allegiance	Robert D. Cornwall	$9.99
History and Christian Faith	Edward W. H. Vick	$9.99
The Church Under the Cross	William Powell Tuck	$11.99
The Journey to the Undiscovered Country	William Powell Tuck	$9.99
Eschatology: A Participatory Study Guide	Edward W. H. Vick	$9.99

Ministry

Clergy Table Talk	Kent Ira Groff	$9.99
Out of This World	Darren McClellan	$24.99

Generous Quantity Discounts Available
Dealer Inquiries Welcome
Energion Publications — P.O. Box 841
Gonzalez, FL_ 32560
Website: http://energionpubs.com
Phone: (850) 525-3916